FRRLS-PT   JUV 9/17

W9-AWT-840

The life of Aretha Franklin : queen
soul

No levels available

PEACHTREE CITY
PLAN TO STAY™

PEACHTREE CITY LIBRARY
201 Willowbend Road
Peachtree City, GA 30269-1623
Phone: 770-631-2520
Fax: 770-631-2522

PEACHTREE CITY
PLAN TO STAY

PEACHTREE CITY LIBRARY
201 Willowbend Road
Peachtree City, GA 30269 1623
Phone: 770 631 2520
Fax: 770 631 2522

THE LIFE OF

ARETHA FRANKLIN

Queen of Soul

Series Consultant:
Dr. Russell L. Adams, Chairman
Department of Afro-American Studies, Howard University

Silvia Anne Sheafer

Enslow Publishers, Inc.
40 Industrial Road
Box 398
Berkeley Heights, NJ 07922
USA
http://www.enslow.com

Copyright © 2015 by Silvia Anne Sheafer

All rights reserved.

Originally published as *Aretha Franklin: Motown Superstar* in 1996.

No part of this book may be reproduced by any means
without the written permission of the publisher.

Library of Congress Cataloging-in-Publication Data

Sheafer, Silvia Anne.
    The life of Aretha Franklin : queen of soul / Silvia Anne Sheafer.
        pages cm. — (Legendary African Americans)
    "Originally published as: Aretha Franklin : Motown Superstar in 1996."
    Includes bibliographical references and index.
    ISBN 978-0-7660-6225-2
    1. Franklin, Aretha—Juvenile literature. 2. Soul musicians—United States—Biography—Juvenile
literature. 3. African American musicians—Biography—Juvenile literature. I. Title.
    ML3930.F68S53 2014
    782.421644092—dc23
    [B]
                      2014026894

Future editions:
Paperback ISBN: 978-0-7660-6226-9
EPUB ISBN: 978-0-7660-6227-6
Single-User PDF ISBN: 978-0-7660-6228-3
Multi-User PDF ISBN: 978-0-7660-6229-0

Printed in the United States of America
102014 Bang Printing, Brainerd, Minn.
10 9 8 7 6 5 4 3 2 1

To Our Readers:
We have done our best to make sure all Internet Addresses in this book were active and appropriate when we
went to press. However, the author and the publisher have no control over and assume no liability for the
material available on those Internet sites or on other Web sites they may link to. Any comments or
suggestions can be sent by e-mail to comments@enslow.com or to the address on the back cover.

♻ Enslow Publishers, Inc., is committed to printing our books on recycled paper. The paper in every
book contains 10% to 30% post-consumer waste (PCW). The cover board on the outside of each book
contains 100% PCW. Our goal is to do our part to help young people and the environment too!

Illustration Credit: ©ASSOCIATED PRESS (Photo by Peter Kramer), p. 4.

Cover Credit: ©ASSOCIATED PRESS (Photo by Peter Kramer)

CONTENTS

Aretha Franklin at the 61st Annual Tony Awards held in New York City on June 13, 2010.

Chapter 1

ROCKING IN THE ROSE GARDEN

A retha Franklin, the legendary "Queen of Soul," stood anxiously under the extended green tent blanketing the beautiful White House Rose Garden. For her, June 20, 1994, would be a memorable day. Musical producers checked last-minute details and members of the elite international press corps sauntered about. They commented on recent activities of President Bill Clinton, the last time they were in the garden, and Franklin's attire. She was known to dress flamboyantly, even garishly. Performing for President Clinton during his 1993 inaugural festivities, Franklin wore what one reporter referred to as "a fur that may stand as the Pearl Harbor of the animal-rights movement."[1] But on June 20 she was every inch the "Queen of Soul," wearing a white silk gown embroidered with translucent beads and real pearls, and a regal train befitting a reigning monarch. She was a queen in a classical garden. Performing with her was veteran bluesman and balladeer Lou Rawls.

As one hundred and fifty privileged guests were ushered to their seats—eyes shifted from the superstars to the awaited entrance of President and Mrs. Clinton. In the background musicians tuned their instruments, piano keys tinkled. Television sound and camera crews adjusted their equipment. A gentle breeze meandered through the garden, ruffling creamy white rose petals and deep pink geraniums. Looking south one could see the sparkling lights focusing on the Ellipse (a tree-bordered circle due south of the White House) and the Washington Monument. And like a magnificent centurion in the far corner of the garden, an enormous magnolia stood, planted in the early 1830s by President Andrew Jackson.

A stellar White House guest list of music lovers of all ages rounded out the event. Guests included Commerce Secretary Ron Brown; Reverend Jesse Jackson; Representative Bobby Rush of Illinois; and Dennis Archer, the mayor of Franklin's Detroit hometown. It was in Detroit that the timid, little, African-American girl once stood on a chair to sing gospel in her father's Baptist church. Now she sang for the President of the United States.

A bygone melody summed Franklin's amazing and hard-won success. Her father, the late Reverend C. L. Franklin, had often sung it to her as a child. "Look to the Rainbow" again captured the essences of her life.

As the festivities were about to begin inside the Rose Garden tent, the mood suddenly became electric. The crowd was on its feet. In strolled President Clinton, who smiled enthusiastically to the audience and then acknowledged

Franklin. He proclaimed her to be "already a part of American musical history" and said that she had a "genius for moving an audience with her sincerity, her passion, and her grace."[2]

Franklin then stepped onto center stage. She moved naturally through the blinding television lights. Her regal costume glittered under the glare. She leaned back and let her rich resonant voice pour forth in song, taking her audience on a musical journey back to her roots. These were songs she knew well. Some she had written herself and some she had sung in her father's church. At times the audience sang with her, and always, there was enthusiastic clapping.

When she sang "Brand New Me," Franklin rocked so hard that she lost a shoe crossing the stage. For "Ol' Man River" she cooled to a dirge-like pace. She scatted over swinging "I Want To Be Happy," and sang "Cottage for Sale" as a moody ballad. The musicians unexpectedly left the stage when Franklin brought out Lou Rawls. "We don't need 'em," she said, sitting down at the keyboard.[3] She imitated a boogie-woogie bass for their rendition of "Tobacco Road." The audience went wild. Like the soul goddess she was called, her voice rose and drowned the ovation. At one point she leaned forward and peered deep into Bill Clinton's eyes, singing "Smile (Though You Feel Like Crying)." Before long, Clinton was swaying to "Drink to Me Only With Thine Eyes."

The evening reached its climax with a special tribute to the President and Mrs. Clinton. Honed from her gospel background, Franklin's knack for sensitive and poetic lyrics befitting an occasion is one of her finer talents. This quality was obvious with her tribute song to the President. With the

Washington, D.C., Eastern High School choir as backup, Franklin dedicated "Tomorrowland," from one of her favorite motion pictures—*An Affair to Remember*. Franklin brought the President and the audience to their feet with this beautiful version of the Harry Warren and Harold Adamson song.

Franklin, Rawls, and the high school choir ended the one-hour set with a rousing "I Was Born To Sing the Gospel." Now in her early fifties, the African-American girl from New Bethel Baptist Church in Detroit had truly taken her place in American history.

This was not the first time Franklin had been asked to sing at the White House. According to Mary Ann French of the *Washington Post*:

> She has vague memories of Marvin Hamlisch making overtures some time back for her to join in with a group of other presidential entertainers. It wasn't a bit part, but it wasn't front and center either. It apparently took Bill Clinton to pay proper homage to the queen, offering to host her in the intimate Rose Garden setting.[4]

"Well, they said he was a bubba, didn't they?" Franklin fired back to reporters' questions the day before the concert. "I think he's very down to earth, very decent. That's the impression I get. Someone who is really trying to pull it off, to get a true democracy."[5]

The night before her Rose Garden appearance, Franklin appeared at the Kennedy Center Concert Hall. She sang, without pay, to help raise money for the Congressional Black Caucus Spouses' scholarship fund.

Despite acoustical variations at the concert hall, the crowd was loyal, jumping to its feet repeatedly for the superstar. Franklin did her part, dipping and shimmying through her mega-hits—"Chain of Fools," "Freeway of Love," and "Respect," for which she received two 1967 Grammy awards.

Her other career highlights have included a role in the 1980 comedy film *The Blues Brothers* with Dan Ackroyd and John Belushi. Franklin played a waitress in the Maxwell Street soul kitchen, singing a new version of her 1969 Number 1 hit song "Think." She became one of the highlights of the movie. She did a Royal Command Performance for Queen Elizabeth II of England, with Sammy Davis hosting. And later she landed a feature-film role, starring with Ann Margaret. They played "pen pals" who had not seen each other. Franklin quipped to USA Today, "When we do meet, she's in shock to find I'm a black woman."[6]

Stardom had rocked Franklin up and down and back— from gospel to MTV, from segregated restaurants and hotel rooms to the White House. Two husbands, the death of three loved ones within a year, the exhausting bus rides from one engagement to another, the professional battles to stay on top—all had a profound influence on her artistic talents.

Her songs spoke of heartbreak, unbridled passion, and her love for God. Her singing was always charged with emotion and blistering honesty. Reverend Robert Smith, Jr., who replaced her father as pastor at New Bethel, once told a reporter, "You look in her eyes and you see sorrow. I guess that's what makes her such a soulful singer."[7]

Through all Franklin's personal turmoil, she has recorded fifty-eight albums, released seventeen top-ten singles (more than any other female singer in pop history), and won fifteen Grammys (more than any other female performer ever).

She received the Grammy Lifetime Achievement Award in 1994, and made classic records in almost every category. Franklin supported and sang at events taking place during the civil rights movement, and in 1988 supported Reverend Jesse Jackson for President. One of her greatest hours came when Dr. Martin Luther King, Jr., bestowed upon her a special award for support of the Southern Christian Leadership Council (SCLC). One of Dr. King's favorite songs was "Precious Lord." Whenever they were together King asked Franklin to sing it for him. In April 1968 Franklin sang "Precious Lord" for Dr. King one last time, at his funeral in Atlanta. Long ago dubbed the "Queen of Soul," Franklin is, indeed, a music legend. Aretha Franklin's name in African-American culture "holds near-mythic resonance," said journalist James T. Jones, IV, in *Vanity Fair*.[8]

Chapter 2

BACK TO THE BEGINNING

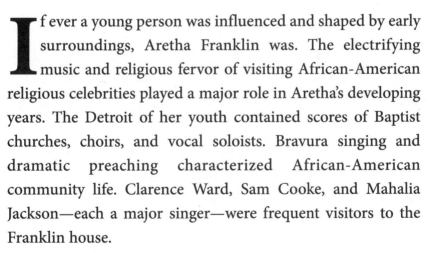

I f ever a young person was influenced and shaped by early surroundings, Aretha Franklin was. The electrifying music and religious fervor of visiting African-American religious celebrities played a major role in Aretha's developing years. The Detroit of her youth contained scores of Baptist churches, choirs, and vocal soloists. Bravura singing and dramatic preaching characterized African-American community life. Clarence Ward, Sam Cooke, and Mahalia Jackson—each a major singer—were frequent visitors to the Franklin house.

"Gospel music is nothing but singing of good tidings straight from the human heart," Mahalia Jackson, herself a gospel great, once said.[1] As a friend and frequent visitor to the Franklin household, Jackson's simple explanation for her emotionally charged singing had deeper meaning.

Like Mahalia Jackson, Aretha Franklin would have her share of troubles. And like Jackson, she met them head-on. Heartache, racial prejudice, unhappy marriages—she tackled them with religious conviction. Aretha was gifted with an expressive five-octave singing voice. Personal drama and a flamboyant image also helped. These were impressionable years for young Aretha.

Aretha Louise Franklin was born March 25, 1942, in Memphis, Tennessee. She was the fourth of five children in a family of three girls and two boys. Her father, Clarence LaVaughn Franklin, was a charismatic Baptist minister and gospel singer. Her mother, Barbara Siggers Franklin, was also a talented gospel singer. When Franklin was two years old, the family moved to Buffalo, New York. Five years later the Franklins settled in Detroit, Michigan. It was there that Reverend Clarence LaVaughn Franklin became pastor of the forty-five hundred seat New Bethel Baptist Church. The church became an outlet for many nationally known gospel singers.

Reverend Franklin was born in 1915 in rural Mississippi. He had a natural flair for expressive preaching, and in Detroit, he made his name and reputation. "The Reverend C. L. Franklin was no ordinary minister," wrote James T. Jones, IV, of *Vanity Fair:*

In the black culture of the segregated 40s, 50s, and 60s, the preacher carried enormous social and political influence. C. L. Franklin was one of the country's most powerful black pastors, a man who attempted to organize his own northern version of the Southern Christian Leadership Conference, a passionate, ambitious leader. . . . a voice that could wrap itself around the deepest, most private feelings of his thousands of parishioners.[2]

He was a spellbinding preacher.

Columbia record producer John Hammond had a different opinion. "Aretha's mother was one of the really great gospel singers. . . . who had more talent than Reverend C. L. Franklin."[3] Which parent had the more natural gift for singing gospel is unimportant; the household was continually infused with religious harmony and famous performers such as Mahalia Jackson, Clara Mae Ward, and Sam Cooke.

Mahalia Jackson was certainly a prime influence on young Aretha. Hailed as the world's greatest gospel singer, Jackson's rich contralto voice was a familiar sound in the Franklin home. By the late 1950s her gospel records, such as "Move On Up a Little," sold in the millions. Throughout America she had her own radio show. She had toured Europe, winning the French Academy's Grand Prix du Disque for "Let the Holy Ghost Fall on Me." Jackson's deep faith in God and the profound emotions she gave to her music were feelings Aretha would someday give to her music.

When Aretha was ten, her mother died. "Reverend Franklin was gone so much," commented a friend.[4] Aretha does not talk about the loss of her mother. Other women soon stepped into the Franklin household—housekeepers and entertainers— attempting to fulfill the children's needs. Clara Mae Ward was a colorful and well-known African-American performer who sang gospel. She was a frequent guest at the Franklins. Her success in the music world had drawn national attention in

1957. When Ward took her five "Famous Ward Singers," on a gospel-singing tour of the South, it was national news. *Newsweek* magazine reported:

> Borne along in a cream-colored limousine with eight doors, costumed from a richly colored wardrobe worth $50,000, "The Big Gospel Cavalcade of '57" stopped at a different city, where they poured out their rhythmic music to audiences with a hunger for it.[5]

When asked why gospel singing was becoming so popular Ward replied:

> I think it fills a vacuum in people's lives. For people who work hard and make little money it offers a promise that things will be better in the life to come. It's like in slavery times, it cheers the downtrodden. It came from our people in our churches. My mother was a gospel singer . . . and she taught me to sing when I was 5 years old. I didn't expect to make a living this way.[6]

By then it was more than a living for Clara Mae Ward; it was an industry. *Newsweek* reported:

> Last year, the Ward Singers grossed half a million dollars. [Ward's] records have sold several million copies, she owns the Ward House of Music in Philadelphia, and since [their beginning, she and the group] have traveled 900,000 miles a year and worn out fifteen automobiles.[7]

This was a significant accomplishment for the thirty-four-year-old African-American gospel singer in the 1950s, and certainly a fascinating role model for Aretha.

When Aretha Franklin was eight she began studying piano. Her father encouraged her and hired a teacher to give her lessons. Aretha refused the lessons. "When she'd come I'd hide. She had the baby piano books and I wanted to go directly to the tunes."[8] The piano lessons did not last long. Aretha soon learned to play piano by ear. Occasionally she received instruction from musicians, such as the Reverend James Cleveland, who performed frequently at her father's church.

Known by titles such as "King James" and the "Crown Prince," Cleveland emerged as a giant of the postwar gospel music scene. Likened to the vocal style of Louis Armstrong, his raw bluesy growls and shouts appeared on more recordings than any other gospel singer of his generation. Like Clara Mae Ward and Mahalia Jackson, he began his training in church. Cleveland later studied piano and joined the Gospelaires trio. By the 1950s he was performing with artists such as Mahalia Jackson, the Thorn Gospel Singers, and the Mediation Singers. He still found time to help teach Aretha piano.

Another favorite houseguest was gospel singer Sam Cooke, the son of a Baptist minister. By 1950 he was the lead singer for the renowned gospel group the Soul Stirrers. In 1957 he recorded "You Send Me," which climbed to Number 1 on the rhythm and blues chart. He taught Aretha how to play chords and reach the high notes. "Sam was the best singer who ever lived, no contest," record producer Jerry Wexler once said.

Singer Rod Stewart described Cooke's influence on him as being so profound he spent two years listening only to his music.[9]

Popular musicians such as singers Lou Rawls, Dorothy Donegan, and B.B. King also played a part in Aretha's future success. There was always music in the Franklin house:

> The radio was going in one room, the record player in another, the piano banging away in the living room. . . . Mahalia would come in, put a pot of greens on the stove, sit around and talk and eat. . . . And something would start up.[10]

Aretha's first big day came at age twelve. Although she was a shy child, Aretha stood on a little chair and sang her first solo in her father's church. She also played piano in the church, and with her sister, Erma, joined a gospel quartet directed by Reverend James Cleveland. Like a sudden shooting star, Aretha had made a hit with the parishioners. When she was singing with the church choir as a soloist she made $15 a week.

"Good gospel really swings," Clara Mae Ward once told a journalist:

> It's from the heart. It gets you so much all over you, you just can't be still. You just can't imagine what it's like. But we don't just sing music that has no meaning. Our songs plead for sinners just like Billy Graham does in Madison Square Garden.[11]

Aretha was demonstrating all those feelings and she knew she wanted to be like Clara Mae Ward. "Clara knocked me out. From then on, I knew I wanted to sing."[12]

Aretha learned all the songs of famous singers, and even played the piano like them. She also enjoyed watching boxing matches on television—especially famous boxers such as Ray Robinson, Rocky Marciano, and Joe Louis. Other times she was just another little girl who liked to roller skate and eat ice cream. She played piano, and with her sisters and friends, sang all the popular songs of the day. She admired jazz pianist Art Tatum, saying "the way he could just sit down and play. I just canceled that out for me and knew that I could never do that, but he left a strong impression on me, as a pianist and a person."[13]

Of all those who gave her inspiration, Aretha said that her father had the greatest impact on her. The way her father combined his preaching and his music really impressed her. As she herself put it, "Most of what I learned vocally came from him. He gave me a sense of timing in music and timing is important in everything."[14]

The growing Franklin family lived in a big house in Detroit, shaded by trees and with a fine backyard. Despite living in the inner city the Franklin children all seemed to stay away from its negative aspects. "We were very good kids," Aretha said.[15]

When Aretha was fourteen she cut her first album. Chess Records had recorded her father's sermons, and it seemed natural that they would have her cut *Songs of Faith*. These spirituals and hymns, including "Never Grow Old" and "There Is a Fountain Filled With Blood," are all-time favorites. This album of emotionally powerful songs helped to establish Aretha Franklin as a young gospel singer to be taken seriously.

About this time Reverend Franklin's career began to expand. He was signed to do a radio show, preaching the gospel to those who could not attend church. His sermons were recorded on LPs (long- playing records) and distributed nationwide. He was able to organize his own traveling revival show, complete with a choir and gospel singers. At fourteen Aretha left school to go on the road with Franklin's Gospel Caravan, an endless tour in which the family traveled thousands of miles by car.

Chapter 3

"PRECIOUS LORD"

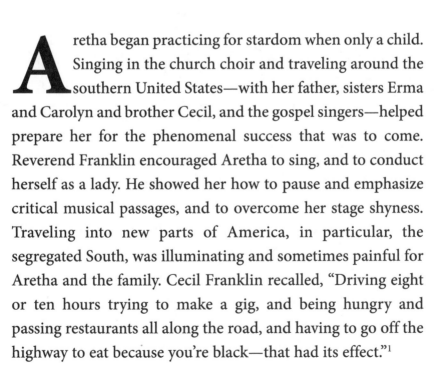

Aretha began practicing for stardom when only a child. Singing in the church choir and traveling around the southern United States—with her father, sisters Erma and Carolyn and brother Cecil, and the gospel singers—helped prepare her for the phenomenal success that was to come. Reverend Franklin encouraged Aretha to sing, and to conduct herself as a lady. He showed her how to pause and emphasize critical musical passages, and to overcome her stage shyness. Traveling into new parts of America, in particular, the segregated South, was illuminating and sometimes painful for Aretha and the family. Cecil Franklin recalled, "Driving eight or ten hours trying to make a gig, and being hungry and passing restaurants all along the road, and having to go off the highway to eat because you're black—that had its effect."[1]

Racial prejudice had always been much more prevalent in the southern states than in the North. Until 1954, when the United States Supreme Court ruled that segregation in public education was unconstitutional, many African-American children received limited schooling. African Americans were unable to enter the professional job market. Particularly in the South, many whites practiced segregation, or separation of black from whites:

> The plight of the nation's poor blacks seemed especially bleak. Ever since emancipation, blacks in both North and South had faced discrimination in jobs, housing, education, and other areas. A lack of education and jobs made poverty among blacks widespread.[2]

African-American families often had trouble finding adequate living quarters. Some property owners refused to sell or rent to them. In 1948 the Supreme Court ruled on this— that protective covenants, or agreements, not to sell to African Americans were illegal. But in the South these laws were not enforced. Black families had poorer living conditions than whites. Restaurants refused to serve African Americans; and for blacks, riding a bus sometimes meant sitting in the back seats.

African-American musicians as well as ordinary blacks felt the ugly squeeze of racial prejudice. But the hope of stopping segregation and insuring African-American equality was about to come. A young Baptist minister named Martin Luther King, Jr., emerged as a civil rights leader after a bus boycott in Montgomery, Alabama. Singer Dinah Washington did free benefits and often sent money to aid King's various causes. She told her friend LaRue Manns, "I may not see it, but someday things will be better."[3] Dinah Washington always believed racial discrimination would change, and that some day she would be able to walk into a hotel and have a nice suite and go sit in the dining room.

Growing support came from many African Americans. Those who fought against segregation would soon lead the civil rights movement. In the 1950s Reverend Franklin and his touring gospel caravans had suffered undue racial prejudice, especially in the South. When they met other African-American entertainers along the way, Reverend Franklin befriended them. When these entertainers came to Detroit, the Franklin home was a welcome stop. Reverend Franklin would have dinner fixed for them, and his guests would spend the night. Often this lead to singing—with everyone joining in.

Young Aretha had a way of taking someone else's recordings, altering them, and making them her own. The music of blues singer Bessie Smith and Clara Mae Ward were special favorites. Smith's particular language was the classic material of all blues singers—poverty, oppression, quiet pain, and love. She recorded the all-time classic *Down Hearted Blues* for Columbia Records in 1923. It became an enormous success, selling more than 2 million records. During the 1930s Smith sang at Harlem's Apollo Theater in New York and the Newark Opera House, now the New Jersey State Opera House. But her appearance at Manhattan's Connie's Inn, later called the Latin Quarter, lasted only three nights.

Record producer John Hammond wrote in his biography, "Bessie just could not sing comfortably for white audiences."[4] Still he considered her the greatest blues singer he had ever heard. He arranged for her to cut more records for Columbia.

During one of her many trips to Huntsville, Alabama, in 1937, the old Packard in which she was driving was forced off the road. Smith's arm was nearly severed. The owner of a tent show, and a witness to the accident, later told Hammond that two ambulances passed her by because she was African American. She died before reaching a hospital. Hammond said that two other witnesses nodded agreement about the story, but when he told them that he was a magazine writer, the one said, "Don't quote me."[5]

In 1971 Columbia put together all the records that Smith had made, and released enough for five double LP albums. Familiar with Smith's tragic death and a great admirer of all her music, Franklin empathized with Bessie Smith and found raw and forceful soul. Franklin's interpretation of "He Will Wash You White as Snow" was reminiscent of Bessie's earlier style.

During the 1950s African-American music and Detroit become synonymous. Although this was prior to Motown Records, Detroit—once primarily known as the automobile capital of the world and later Motor City—echoed with the rich sounds of gospel, and rhythm and blues. Traditional African-American music was capturing the musical hearts and ambitions of many young performers. The Temptations and

Smokey Robinson were headliners. What black musicians were giving a growing white audience was a new kind of music with a unique rhythm and deep-rooted gospel rolled into soul.

"You must make your audience feel what you feel," Sam Cooke once told an interviewer. "If you have ever attended Baptist services, you'll know what I mean. You have to stir up the emotions of the congregation and literally lift them from their chairs."[6]

These young performers, who all came to hear Aretha Franklin perform on Sunday nights at the New Bethel Baptist Church, often helped each other put song and dance together. "It was easy to put out records in those days," said music industry executive Billy Davis:

> In 1956 with $500 you could record it, press it, and take it around to your local radio stations and get it played. You could discover a talent one day, have them in the studio within a week, and have a record out and on the air within two weeks. It was an exciting time in Detroit. All this musical activity helped to keep a lot of kids out of trouble.[7]

At fifteen Aretha not only played a rocking piano, but was becoming a teenage gospel sensation. She often sang with her older sister, Erma, also a "terrific singer" as recalled by Billy Davis. As for Aretha, Davis had only praise. "The impression I had of Aretha, was that she was a child genius. Everything that she sang was with such emotion that you felt every word."[8]

Growing up without a mother's guidance, facing racial prejudice, and traveling in an adult caravan, presented more serious problems for Aretha. At fifteen, still just a child, she became pregnant. She dropped out of school and suddenly found herself in an adult situation. Any plans that she had for a career took second place to the birth of her first child.

Unwed motherhood was not new in the "projects." Girls as young as thirteen and fourteen became unwed mothers before entering high school. But for the daughter of a prominent Baptist minister, pregnancy was a surprise. Who was the father? To this day Franklin does not talk about it nor reveal who he was. What she holds dear is the love for her first son, Clarence.

With days now spent awaiting his arrival, Aretha played the piano, practiced her singing, and arranged music. She also had a new idol—the flamboyant and talented Dinah Washington. Washington often came to Detroit to perform, where she was treated like visiting royalty. She dressed in exquisite gowns and rode in fancy cars. It was during these waiting months and the years of Clarence's infancy, that Dinah Washington came to visit and stay at the Franklin house.

Aretha attended Washington's performances and stood in the back of the theater to hear her perform. This period had a major impact on Franklin and helped her decide on the direction of her career. Still, life without a mother's guidance was tough. Two years later, at seventeen, Aretha gave birth to another son named Edward. She has never revealed his father's name. But she admits motherhood arrived before she was entirely ready for it. "I still wanted to get out and hang with my friends," she said. "So I wanted to be in two places at the same time. But my grandmother helped me a lot, and my sister and my cousin. They would baby-sit so I could get out occasionally."[9]

Aretha continued to practice her singing, and then her big chance came. In 1960 she was encouraged by Major "Mule" Holly, the bassist for the jazz pianist Teddy Wilson. Holly told Aretha that she could become a popular singer. She had a certain style that was salable in jazz or even popular music.[10]

With friends and relatives to help care for the two little boys, Reverend Franklin and Aretha decided to go to New York City. There, they prepared for Franklin's audition. She made "demo" records and went to a special school that helped train and develop her as a star performer. The international musical world was about to hear from the future "Queen of Soul."

According to John Hammond, then a record producer at Columbia Records:

One day a black composer arrived at my office with a demonstration record of various songs he had written. The fourth one particularly caught my ear, partly because it was a good song, partly because it sounded familiar. It was called "Today I Sing the Blues," and performed by a young woman who accompanied herself on the piano. . . . Her name was Aretha Franklin, and even at first hearing, on a poorly made demo intended to sell songs rather than the singer, she was the most dynamic jazz voice I'd encountered since Billie [Holiday.][11]

Franklin had grabbed the attention of her peers.

Chapter 4

Making
It on Record

John Hammond learned that Aretha Franklin, whom he was interested in signing, was from Detroit. He had received a call from Jo King, owner of a small record studio. She told him that Franklin would be in her studio that day. Coincidentally, Sam Cooke, who once had been a member of Reverend Franklin's church choir, was interested in signing her to RCA Records. Hammond won. In 1960 he got Franklin a top royalty contract with Columbia. At the time he wanted to keep much of the gospel feelings in her voice, while using material that would attract jazz fans as well.

Even though Franklin was only eighteen, and a newcomer to the gigantic recording industry, she knew how she wanted to record. She asked Hammond for good, solid, jazz musicians as backup. She would record with five jazz players, asking for a rock drummer as well.

The relationship with Hammond and Columbia Records was a big break for Franklin. She was, after all, a newcomer and unheard of outside Detroit. With a new record contract, she was able to get night club engagements and concert appearances. Franklin attended the opening of Mahalia Jackson's concert at Madison Square Garden in New York City. Jackson recalled that Franklin came to her "all distressed about the first chance she had to cut some little record off from gospel—afraid of what her father would say." Mahalia told her "just ask God's guidance and go on."[1]

"Today I Sing the Blues," released in October 1960, was a mournful blues number, and Franklin's debut single for Columbia. It shot up the R&B (rhythm and blues) charts and became her first top-ten recording. She had established herself as a solid performer, and was an instant hit with the jazz audience. Her second top-ten recording was an upbeat Johnny MacFarland tune, "Won't Be Long." The album was released in 1961 with other hits such as Judy Garland's signature song "Over the Rainbow," "All Night Long," "It Ain't Necessarily So," and "Sweet Lover." From this debut album, Aretha, later came two more re-releases, the second in 1972, called *The Great Aretha Franklin—The First 12 Sides*. *Billboard* magazine was quick to say, "she brings a true and strong gospel accent into a fine full-blown blues."[2]

So impressed with Franklin's first single, Columbia wanted to sign Franklin's sister, Erma, to Columbia's subsidiary label. Although Hammond wrote later that he had nothing to do with signing Erma, this eventually ended his association with Aretha Franklin.[3]

What Franklin was bringing to her recordings was the ability "[to] make other people feel what you're feeling. It's hard to laugh when you want to cry," she said. "Some people can hide it. I can't so when I sing it doesn't come across fake."[4]

During the early years at Columbia, Franklin was traveling between New York and Detroit. It was in Detroit that another famous African-American singer, Della Reese, introduced her to Ted White. Six months later in 1961, Franklin and White were married. He took over the direction of her career. With a growing and successful musical career, Franklin gave birth to her third son, Ted, Jr.

Franklin was on her way to becoming a big name in the music world. She and her jazz combo were headliners at the three-day Newport Jazz Festival in Newport, Rhode Island, in July 1962. Performing alongside the Clara Mae Ward Gospel Singers and Duke Ellington, that same year she also played Las Vegas and clubs in the Caribbean.

Records continued for Franklin, but not all of them were big winners. Yet Hammond claimed that the records produced after she was assigned a new producer were commercial. These singles, using Franklin's voice with a large backup band, were "How Deep Is the Ocean" and "Lover Come Back to Me," and a tribute to Dinah Washington with "Cold, Cold Heart," "What a Diff'rence a Day Makes," "Evil Gal Blues," and "Unforgettable."

Franklin was moved from one producer to another while these lavish records did little to increase her sales and nothing to enhance her career.[5] Franklin was disturbed about the backup music. At the time African-American rhythm-and-blues singers had only limited success in this market. "Black music" was still considered a thing apart, special and different.

In music catalogs African-American music was listed under "race," "ebony," or "sepia." This label told buyers that the records were made for black audiences and made by black singers. White musicians would "borrow" black music and remake records, but no money was paid to the black composer or the black musician who performed it.

Franklin was wavering in both worlds. Her heritage and background were black; Columbia, her recording company, was white. She was dissatisfied with their contractual performance. And she later said, "I was afraid. I sang to the floor a lot."[6]

About this time Columbia decided to have record producer Clyde Otis move Franklin into contemporary music. The explosion of Motown Records and its hot recordings of African-American singers such as The Supremes and Dionne Warwick had introduced an exciting new musical era. Otis and Franklin decided on recording *Runnin' Out of Fools*. Franklin proved that she could handle rock, pop, and R&B material, but album sales fell short. Franklin and Otis blamed this on a lack of promotion on Columbia's part. Even though Franklin had toned down her style, Columbia was not into soulful music. Aside from the music's downsides, Otis and White were not seeing eye-to-eye. It became a matter of style and personalities.

In the end Otis walked away. Franklin's marriage was also not what one would expect. Gospel singer and friend Mavis Staples said, "She fooled round and got with a man like Ted White, but that's the kind of dude Aretha likes, the dude that flies fancy." Willie Todd, a New Bethel Baptist Church deacon, added that "Reverend Franklin couldn't stand Ted." And pianist Teddy Harris agreed, "Aretha is the kind of girl you've got to love hard. She requires a lot of attention and she didn't get that from Ted."[7]

Early success and motherhood, and then tragedy were the things that molded Franklin's sensitive style. In 1963 her idol, Dinah Washington, died from an accidental overdose of pills and alcohol. Stunned by Washington's death, Franklin told the press, "The Queen of the Blues was—and still is—Dinah Washington!" In loving tribute Franklin recorded an album of Dinah's hits—*Unforgettable*. According to one source [the] "album is without a doubt her most artistically successful Columbia LP. . . . Original copies of it are considered prized collector's items, as well as a creative milestone in Aretha's career."[8]

Nearing the end of her contract, Franklin sued Columbia. She received an out-of-court settlement. Columbia has since packaged and repackaged her many hit songs. Almost immediately after her break with Columbia, Franklin signed with Atlantic Records.

At Atlantic Records, Franklin teamed with record producer and senior partner Jerry Wexler. Her first recording, "I Never Loved a Man the Way I Love You," was made on January 27, 1967. It was a night that Jerry Wexler would never forget, nor drummer Roger Hawkins. The minute Franklin touched the piano and sang one note, the musicians were captivated. "I've never experienced so much feeling coming out of one human being," said Hawkins.[9] "When she hit the first chord," added songwriter Dan Penn, "we knew everything was gonna' be all right."[10] It was the recording session that yielded the single record "Respect." This song would make Aretha Franklin an international singing star. On the flip side, Franklin's two sisters, Erma and Carolyn, joined her with "Do Right Woman—Do Right Man." Wexler said that Franklin "over dubbed two discrete keyboard parts, first playing piano, then organ; she and her sisters hemstitched the seamless background harmonies; and when she added her lead vocal, the result was perfection."[11]

Two weeks after the "Do Right Woman—Do Right Man" was sent to radio and record shops, it hit Number 9 on the Pop Record Charts, Number 1 on the R&B charts, and became her first million-seller. If the first single was a success, said Wexler, "the second single was a rocket to the moon. She took Otis Redding's "Respect" and turned it inside out, making it deeper, stronger, loading it with double entendres."[12] Franklin and her sister, Erma, came up with the now famous "sock-it-to-me" line. In a year when other sensational singers such as the Supremes and the Beatles were breaking new records, Franklin was right there with them.

What Wexler had done was to sit her down at the piano, and have her play and sing as she had done in church. Wexler said:

Basically, my idea was to make bluesy, funky records. One of the main things was to put Aretha at the piano. I've always felt that singers who also play instruments, no matter how well or poorly they do it, should always play on their records. Aretha happens to play the piano exceptionally well.[13]

Record producer Jerry Wexler was also a senior partner of R&B Music. He had been watching Franklin for some time, waiting for her contract with Atlantic to expire. Unlike some critics of her earlier records, he said "people are negating some of the beautiful things she did on Columbia . . . ballads . . . show tunes. . . . Wonderful things, like the ballad from *Camelot*, 'If Ever I Should Leave You.'"[14] Wexler continued to acclaim his new singer and later said:

> I'd say she's a musical genius comparable to that other great musical genius, Ray Charles. Both play a terrific gospel piano which is one of the greatest assets one can have today. Since they have this broader talent, they can bring to a recording session a total conception of the music, and thus contribute much more than the average artist.[15]

From 1967 to 1968 Franklin released six top-ten pop singles, including another all-time winner "You Make Me Feel Like a Natural Woman," and three top-ten albums, including *Lady Soul*—which yielded four hits. Five of the singles were certified gold records, and two albums were certified gold. During this time Franklin's recordings tumbled out at the rate of two a year.

"Respect" became Franklin's trademark, topped the charts, and in 1968 ranked in the *Rolling Stone* publication's all-time top ten. Franklin was surely earning her title "Queen of Soul."

On her way to the top, Aretha could have become affected. Instead, she said:

> My dad's responsible for that. . . . Had it not been for him, I would've become affected much younger. I lived in New York for a period of time . . . I would come home to visit, I didn't feel like I should have to share the housework . . . everyone would be working, washing dishes and vacuuming . . . and I would be standing around . . . my dad came downstairs . . . and he said, "See if you can find your way in that kitchen and introduce yourself to the trash."[16]

Chapter 5

THE CIVIL RIGHTS MOVEMENT

B y 1964 Dr. Martin Luther King, Jr., was the most important civil rights leader in America. He headed the Southern Christian Leader- ship Conference (SCLC), headquartered in Atlanta, Georgia. More chapters were being formed in other parts of the United States, but Atlanta remained the center of the movement. Many African-American entertainers had joined King, or were participating in peaceful protests, marches, city-wide boycotts, and sit-ins taking place in large metropolitan areas such as Greensboro, North Carolina, and Birmingham, Alabama.

King was a personal friend of Reverend Franklin and his family. Reverend Franklin was an early advocate of African-American pride and supportive of the civil rights movement.

He invited King to Detroit in 1963. There, King led one hundred and twenty-five thousand people in a great Freedom Walk. He called the event "the largest and greatest demonstration for freedom ever held in the United States."[1] The Freedom Walk was in many respects a rehearsal for the upcoming march on Washington, D.C.

With her new international fame, Franklin had become an inspiring symbol of African-American equality. King enjoyed gospel music. When he was in town, he attended the New Bethel Baptist Church and would ask Franklin to sing "Precious Lord." Franklin not only enjoyed the request from this great individual, but like her father she concurred with Dr. King's goals. "If you believe something is really important," she said, "you should support it."[2]

In Chicago, a young man by the name of Jesse Jackson was also making a name for himself in the civil rights movement. Jackson had been a student leader while attending North Carolina's Agricultural and Technical College. After graduation he told friends that he thought he had been called to preach. He enrolled in Chicago Theological Seminary.[3]

Jackson had a firsthand look at extreme poverty and despair in the Chicago ghetto. According to Jackson biographer Patricia C. McKissack, "He was saddened and angered by the overwhelming waste of human potential. Somehow the cycle had to be broken."[4] To help, he joined the Chicago chapter of the SCLC.

On March 7, 1965, the SCLC organized a march from Selma to Montgomery, Alabama. The purpose was to let people know about the huge African-American voter registration drive taking place, and to urge passage of the voting rights bill before Congress.

It began as a peaceful demonstration. Then violence broke out after Alabama governor George Wallace tried to stop the march. State troopers were called. McKissack wrote:

> The troopers used cattle prods, tear gas, and clubs. Hundreds of demonstrators, including King, were beaten and attacked. King went on television and asked for help. Jesse Jackson saw this plea and was shocked when he saw those cruel acts.[5]

Jackson quickly organized a busload of seminary students and went to Selma. It was at this encounter that he met King.

The following year Jackson organized a nonviolent march, in which King participated, through Chicago's business section. After the protest King placed Jackson in charge of Operation Breadbasket—another nonviolent protest. At age twenty-four, Jackson became the youngest SCLC staff member.

Everything came together for Franklin when she started recording for Atlantic Records. She became the top attraction at college concerts and made guest appearances on prime-time television and glitzy nightclub shows. In 1967 she had won all the major trade awards, and capped off with *Billboard* magazine's citation as the top female singer. The following February, Detroit's mayor Jerome P. Cavanaugh declared "Aretha Franklin Day."

Franklin appeared at a glittering musical performance held in Cobo Hall. Backed up by the Sweet Inspirations, twelve thousand clapping and cheering fans heard her sing. She was honored for her achievements with awards and plaques by all three of the music-trade publications—*Cash Box, Record World,* and *Billboard*—in recognition of her 1967 clean sweep of the music charts. By far her greatest honor came from King. The crowd roared its approval as Dr. King took the stage, giving him a standing ovation. King presented Franklin with a special award from the SCLC, and asked her to sing "Precious Lord." Franklin had become the young symbol of the new African-American woman.

All across the country African Americans were making a dramatic impact. Their pledge for African-American equality was being heard in the streets, on television, and through nonviolent demonstrations. Back in Chicago, Jackson was picketing the A&P Grocery Stores. "Hit them where it hurts the most—in their pocketbooks. Then we'll get their attention," he told the people.[6] His strategy was to boycott businesses that underemployed African Americans or refused to support African-American products. In the beginning these strikes were against only food-producing companies.

Without warning, unexpected tragedy occurred. A garbage workers' strike in Memphis, Tennessee, had turned into a riot. King was asked to come and help. Faced with no other choice, he returned to conduct a peaceful march. Jackson also reported to Memphis. The following morning, April 4, 1968, King spoke briefly to Jackson. "I've looked over and I've seen the Promised Land. I may not get there with you, but I want you to know that we as a people will get to the Promised Land." He asked Jackson to go to dinner with him that night and quipped, "And no blue jeans, all right?"[7] Moments later a loud crack echoed through the air. Dr. Martin Luther King, Jr., had been shot. He was pronounced dead at 7:05 P.M.

Violence erupted in cities from coast to coast. Jackson returned to Chicago. Appearing on television, he used the media to get out his message. "I'm challenging the youth today to be nonviolent as the greatest expression of faith they can make in Dr. King—to put your rocks down, put your battles down."[8] His actions were more in keeping with Dr. King's nonviolent philosophy than the violent action of others.

On April 9 the coffin bearing Dr. Martin Luther King, Jr., was carried through the streets of Atlanta on a crude farm wagon pulled by two Georgian mules. The wagon was followed by tens of thousands of mourners, black and white, in silent tribute to the slain civil rights leader.

Behind the wagon marched some of the nation's highest ranking figures. In the sultry 80° heat Governor Nelson Rockefeller of New York and Senator Robert F. Kennedy made the three and a half mile walk from Ebenezer Baptist Church to an open general service at Morehouse College. Former Vice President Richard Nixon, Vice President Hubert Humphrey, and former First Lady Jacqueline Kennedy were among the mourners. President Lyndon Johnson did not attend.

There were many other public figures in attendance that day, including some from the world of music and theater—Harry Belafonte; Marlon Brando; Bill Cosby; Sammy Davis, Jr.; Ben Gazarra; Barbara McNair; Eartha Kitt; Stevie Wonder; Diana Ross and the Supremes; and Aretha Franklin.

Reverend Ralph Abernathy, a close friend of King's, began the service. "I am the resurrection and the life; he that believeth in Me, though he were dead, yet shall he live."[9] For the next ninety minutes the congregation prayed, wept, and listened to tributes to Dr. King. Most of all they sang.

"It was the soulful part, the hooping, and rhythmic intonation," said the Reverend George W. Lucas, pastor of the Bethel Baptist Church in Dayton, Ohio.[10] Abernathy then interrupted the choir's singing of the gospel hymn "Softly and Tenderly" and urged the congregation to join in. They chanted slowly and quietly. Then, at the end of each verse, the singing swelled to fill the sanctuary with sound. An emotional climax to the service came when Mrs. Mary Gurley, a musical contralto, hands clasped and her eyes closed, sang, "Where He Leads Me." The audience came alive with sobs and shouts of "Oh, yeah" and "Jesus."[11]

Franklin had loved King and supported his nonviolent philosophy. Pulsating emotions peaked as she sang to him one last time.

Following the service, crowds lined the four mile route to the cemetery where Dr. King was buried. The hillside blossomed with dogwood and fresh green boughs. The graveyard was founded in 1866 by six African Americans. Dr. King was buried next to his grandparents. An epitaph on the tombstone, derived from an African-American spiritual read: "Free at last. Free at last. Thank God I'm free at last."

Time to mourn and time to record kept Franklin busy that year. Earlier she recorded "I Can't Get No Satisfaction." Albert Goldman, reviewer for *The New York Times*, said of Franklin:

> She makes salvation seem erotic. The new "Queen of Soul," [with] a finger-popping, hip-swinging Mardi Gras strut that is the greatest proclamation of sexual fulfillment since Molly Bloom's soliloquy. . . . Aretha riffs and rocks and stomps behind, before and on top of the beat, until she and the band are lost in a jam session that might have gone on for hours after the final fade. . . . Although, "Satisfaction" provides the finest vehicle yet found for Aretha's voice and temperament, her more characteristic number is something quite different.[12]

Franklin's impressive road to superstardom was now commanding international notice too. To sell-out and enthusiastic audiences, she toured Europe, appearing in France, Germany, Sweden, and England. Her background singers for the trip were her sister Carolyn, with Wyline Ivey and Charnessa Jones. During her Paris engagement she recorded the album *Aretha in Paris*—thirteen live versions of her songs. Everywhere she appeared, the ovation was overwhelming.

Franklin returned home in August 1968 and opened the Democratic National Convention with her powerful rendition of "The Star-Spangled Banner." It was the same year that she was "officially" crowned "Queen of Soul." It happened during a Chicago performance. A zealous deejay brought out a crown, and from then on the media and her audience began to use the term.

Rhythm and blues hits just kept coming for Franklin. Erma Franklin penned the words to the song "Ain't No Way" and—with Franklin's hot burst of creative energy, and the great sounds of backup singers Cissy Houston and her Sweet Inspirations—the tune hit the pop and R&B charts and was certified gold.

Franklin's fourth album for Atlantic, *Aretha Now*, scored a certified gold. At the end of the year she recorded the single "See Saw." It also was certified gold. It looked as if the "Queen of Soul" could only produce gold.

While Franklin was scoring one hit after another, her friend Jesse Jackson was ordained a minister by the Reverends Franklin and Clay Evans in New Bethel Baptist Church. He has been called Reverend Jesse ever since.

Chapter 6

HAS IT GOT SOUL?

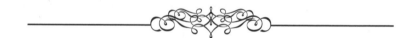

Has it got soul? Man, that's the question of the hour," observed a *Time* magazine music reviewer:

If it has soul, then it's tough, beautiful, out of sight. It passes the test of with-itness. If it has the authenticity of collard greens boiling on the stove, the sassy style of the boogaloo in a hip discothèque, the solidarity signified by "Soul Brother" scrawled on a ghetto storefront. . . . It's like electricity![1]

Wrapped into the reviewers' hype was Aretha Franklin, now twenty-six, riding the soulful pinnacle of the music world. Soul was happening everywhere:

In esthetics and anthropology, history and dietetics, haberdashery and politics—although Hubert Humphrey's recent declaration to college students that he was a "soul brother" was all wrong. Soul is letting *others* say you're a soul brother.[2]

Soul was pop music, the rumble of gospel choirs and the plaintive cry of the blues. Mahalia Jackson had called gospel "a powerful beat, a rhythm we held on to from slavery days."[3] Franklin had been nurtured with its essence. Since her early days of singing in her father's church choir, Franklin had compounded it with the raw emotion, pulsing rhythm, and her unique earthly lyrics. To this musical style she now adopted sparkling sequined gowns and exotic wigs. Her image was undergoing a radical change, and music reviewers were writing with more intensity.

Singing from the stage of a packed Philharmonic Hall in Manhattan, music critics acclaimed Franklin's interpretation of soul with powerful words:

She leaned her head back, forehead gleaming with perspiration, features twisted by her intensity, and her voice—plangent and supple—pierces the hall. "Oh baby what, you done to me," not only captured the senses of the reviewer, but a rollicking audience shouted and clapped, "Tell it like it is!"[4]

Then Franklin moved into another of her great hits— "Respect," moving the audience with earthy candor and the sounds of wailing soul. Not only did it please the audience, "Respect," earned her the first of her many Grammy awards.

"Sock it to me," one of Franklin's variations on "whip it," was another in the long list of sexual terms from blues to jazz that had passed into respectable everyday language. It originated as a catch phrase on the television show *Laugh-In* of the 1960s.

Franklin told *Time* magazine in January 1968, "My music is me—and I'm not sure what that is." Although she claimed she was a shy girl who regarded the glamorous trappings of show business as "a game," she overcame her nervousness at singing in public only by imagining that she is "just at a party, and the audience is just my friends."[5]

"It took years to feel that naturalness before a large audience." As she put it:

> What has happened is that over the years I've gained enough experience to work anywhere and to relate to people on all levels. I know I've improved my overall look and sound; they're much better. And I've gained a great deal of confidence in myself. I wonder how many people know I once had this big problem about actually walking out on the stage . . . all those people sitting out there looking at me, checking me out from head to toe. Wow! That really used to get to me; but I've overcome most of that by just walking out on the stage night after night.[6]

As *Time* magazine described:

> Her singing is something else. . . . She belts out the lyrics in knowing tones of an older and wiser woman. Her plangent voice, ranging from a sensual whisper to a banshee wail—or a

44

throbbing despair and resignation. Adapting the gospel sound of Clara Ward adding the jazz feeling of the Dinah Washington, laying it over a pounding piano rhythm-and-blues beat, she seals it with her own down-home conviction. "Yeah!" she shouts in mid-lyric. "I believe it!"[7]

Franklin often went to the recording sessions having already written her music. She knew the sounds that she wanted. And the group that often sang backup were Erma and Carolyn. Their voices were sometimes dubbed in later.

"Everybody who's living has problems and desires just as I do," Franklin commented about her sensitive lyrics. "When the fellow on the corner has somethin' botherin' him, he feels the same way I do. When we cry, we all gonna' cry tears; and when we laugh, we all have to smile."[8]

Franklin was by all definitions a superstar. Where was there to go but up? Fame had come very fast for this young singer, working mom, and wife. "There was not enough care in the early days with respect to what my schedule was," she told *Vanity Fair*.[9] She became physically and mentally exhausted. Tragic deaths had claimed friends such as Dr. King and his younger brother, Alfred, who drowned in a pool accident. In 1969 Franklin divorced White. An engagement was broken off between Franklin and Dennis Edwards, formerly of the Temptations. "Dennis Edwards was 15 years too late," she said later. "by the time he realized the value of what he had, it was just too late. I was no longer interested." Franklin did not understand why men were afraid of her. "I would never dog anyone," she said. "I would never do that to my man. In fact, I could appreciate a man who appreciates me and who appreciates women."[10]

Despite Franklin's problems with men, her great gospel sounds and rhythm and blues music never stopped satisfying fans. Performing background vocals in many of these hit records was Cissy Houston (Whitney Houston's mother) and her Sweet Inspirations. The group started appearing with Franklin in 1965 at Columbia Records, and in 1967 with the Atlantic album *Aretha Arrives*. "The Sweet Inspirations began in the Atlantic Church of Sixties Soul," said Jerry Wexler. "They instinctively understood harmonies; they could match vibratos, switch parts, and turn on a dime. And they were always relaxed, fun . . ."[11] They performed with other groups as well, and sang background on Elvis Presley's hit song "Suspicious Minds." The group's "Sweet Inspirations" recording was a top-twenty hit.

During recording sessions in New York City with Franklin, Cissy Houston would bring daughter Whitney to the studio. The little girl would peer through the glass, and watch her mother and Franklin sing. "I'd be talking to Aunt Ree. I had no idea then that Aretha Franklin was famous—just that I liked to hear her sing too! . . . I could feel her emotional delivery so clearly. . . . That's what I wanted to do," she recalled.[12] In many interviews thereafter Whitney Houston spoke of Franklin as her inspiration.

In 1970 all four singles released by Franklin became top-ten hits on the R&B charts, including "Call Me," "Spirit in the Dark," "Don't Play That Song for Me," and "Border Song." But the producers, and Franklin, wanted a hit record that would not only become a R&B smash, but would cross over to the pop charts as well. She had not had a top-ten album in two years. As she told Jerry Wexler, "I'm a workin' mother, and I have to pay my bills."[13]

Franklin, now twenty-eight, was set to appear at the Fillmore West Theater in San Francisco. To offset the gate receipts, Atlantic Records decided to have her cut a live album. Her music was rock and roll and a rocking version of some Franklin classics. Wexler had doubts about how she would be received. The San Francisco showplace had been playing host to rockers such as Joe Cocker and the Grateful Dead:

> I considered the musical tastes of the Flower Children infantile and retarded, but I was dead wrong; they were swinging from the rafters, swarming the stage, packed beyond capacity. It was thrilling to see the King Curtis Band backing her. The rhythm section was cooking on high flame.[14]

Franklin wailed with "Respect," and "Love the One You're With." Then she mellowed for Simon and Garfunkel's "Bridge Over Troubled Water" and the Beatles all-time masterpiece "Eleanor Rigby." The audience was totally overcome when Franklin appeared on stage with Ray Charles in tow. They sang and played "Spirit in the Dark," and the crowd went wild.

According to Jerry Wexler, "All I could do was sit there and weep."[15]

Later, Franklin would call the Fillmore concert a highlight of her career. What overwhelmed her—and surprised Wexler—was the musical intelligence of the hippies. "They picked up on her every shading and nuance . . . and were hip to exactly what was happening, technically and emotionally."[16] *Aretha Live at Fillmore West* became a top-ten album in 1971 and a certified gold album. She was back on top!

Chapter 7

"Amazing Grace"

With the huge success of the three-day Fillmore West concert, Franklin's musical status once more zoomed to the top of the entertainment world. Album sales and musical reviews were sensational. Jerry Wexler summed it all up when he wrote:

> To my way of thinking there are three qualities that make a great singer—head, heart, and throat. The head is the intelligence, the phrasing. The heart is the emotionality that feeds the flames. The throat is the chops, the voice. Aretha, though, like Sam Cooke, has all three qualities. Her gift seems to have sprung, like Minerva, full-fledged from Jupiter's head.[1]

Franklin's public was still clapping and cheering over the soul singer's triumph in Manhattan's Philharmonic Hall. The song they were chanting to her was the Franklin perennial, "You Make Me Feel Like a Natural Woman."

There was also a down-home side to Franklin:

> Cooking-up-a-storm . . . arriving in the studio with baskets of homemade chicken, ribs, and ham hocks. Or Aretha leaving the presidential suite of the Fountainbleau in Miami to hang out in the neighborhood with R&B deejay pal Fat Daddy, who hipped her to the best pig's-feet joint back of town. Back at the hotel walking through the opulent lobby and the damp pig's feet spilling out of the take-out bag all over the carpet. Aretha didn't miss a beat. She kept on walking, straight into the elevator and up to her room.[2]

Yet there was also tragedy in Franklin's life. And when it happens it can lay heavy on the heart. In 1971 Franklin's friend and great saxophonist King Curtis was murdered. Curtis had been playing saxophone on Franklin's recordings since 1967. But at the peak of his solo career, Curtis was stabbed to death in New York City by a drug addict. At the funeral service in St. Peter's Lutheran church, Franklin let it all out and sang her version of Clara Mae Ward's "Never Grow Old." The Kingpins and the Memphis Horns played a mournful tribute to him too.

Franklin's most highly acclaimed album of the 1970s, also certified gold soon after, ironically was not only a collection of popular rock and roll hits, but showed the "black pride" phase of her career. The five hit singles she recorded in 1971 on the *Young, Gifted and Black* album were Elton John's "Border Song (Holy Moses)," The Beatles' "The Long and Winding Road," Otis Redding's "I've Been Loving You Too Long," and the signature number, Nina Simone's "Young, Gifted and Black."

Not only did the album do well, it reflected the personal interest she was showing in the African-American revolution sweeping the country. According to her statements, "I believe that the black revolution certainly forced me and the majority of black people to begin taking a second look at ourselves. . . . the revolution influenced me a great deal . . ."[3]

Romance entered Franklin's life again. This time it was with her former road manager, Ken Cunningham. She and Cunningham moved to a large brownstone in New York City. Though they did not marry, their union produced Franklin's fourth son, Kecalf, in 1970.

In 1972 Franklin went back to her musical roots—the church. This time it was to record her deeply moving, live gospel album *Amazing Grace*. It was logical that gospel was a soundtrack to the civil rights movement, both in the form of the hymns sung on the march and in the distant echoes of church music heard in the R&B hits of the day. Jerry Wexler and Asrif Mardin shared coproducing credit with Franklin. The album was to be recorded live at the New Temple Missionary Baptist Church in Los Angeles on two consecutive nights.

Franklin had not recorded in church for eight years and had mixed feelings about doing so. Commenting about the event, she said, "It's a feeling you get there you just don't get anywhere else."[4] Still Franklin had doubts about singing in church. She was afraid members of the Baptist religion would take offense. There was a feeling at the time that people who left the church to sing the "devil's music" could not come back. When Sam Cooke went "pop" he never returned to sing another gospel song. He was worried that gospel fans would think he "was forsaking them and the Lord." His father, a minister, sealed the issue. "Sam, the Lord gave you a voice to make people happy. . . . Go ahead and sing."[5]

Franklin wanted to perform in church and arrangements were completed. Among the audience members were Reverend Franklin, Clara Mae Ward, and John Hammond. Franklin was the lead vocalist, with Reverend James Cleveland directing, and the Southern California Community Choir backing her up. Cleveland also sang backup on the traditional gospel hymn "Precious Memories."

Jerry Wexler, who had been after Franklin to return and sing in church, was in the front row of the New Temple Missionary Baptist Church in Los Angeles, listening to her sing. "We had gone from the Flower Children to the Saints," he said, "and the transition could not have been more successful. . . . Aretha was on fire!"[6]

A secular rhythm section was composed of Cornell Dupree, Richard Tee, Chuck Rainey, Bernard Purdie, and Latin percussionist Pancho Morales. Reverend Franklin had encouraged and inspired his daughter beyond human limits. She sang a medley from "Precious Lord Take My Hand," "You've Got A Friend," Marvin Gaye's "Wholly Holy," a powerful version of Clara Mae Ward's "How I Got Over," the

Rodgers and Hammerstein hit "You'll Never Walk Alone," and a ten-minute rendition of "Amazing Grace." One biographer wrote:

> "Amazing Grace" brought Franklin's past, present, and future all together in a two-record set . . . it was going to crystallize her gospel-singing background into an overwhelming successful album; in fact, it was to become the most successful gospel album ever recorded![7]

Her body and voice were filled with religious conviction as she slowly and effectively recited from the Twenty-Third Psalm as part of the song "Give Yourself to Jesus." In addition to the tremendous success of Franklin's return to church, she was photographed on the album cover wearing a traditional African woman's dashiki-style gown, and a tall head wrap of the same beautiful cloth. *Amazing Grace* won Franklin her eighth Grammy award in the category of "Best Soul Gospel," and went gold. *A New York Times* music critic wrote that *Amazing Grace* was "among her finest achievements."[8]

In an interview with *Ebony* magazine, author Charles L. Sanders asked Franklin, "Retha, we've got all of these 'Jesus People' running around today. I suppose they're just discovering God. What about you? You really think there might be a God or anything like that?"

Franklin's answer was straightforward:

> Well, I don't know about anybody else, but I believe in Him. If I didn't I wouldn't be saying prayers like I do. Now, I don't want to sound phony about this, for I feel a real *kinship* with God

and that's what has helped me pull out of the problems I've faced. Anybody who has kept up with my career knows that I've had my share of problems and trouble, but look at me today. I'm here. I have my health, I'm strong, I have my career and my family and plenty of friends everywhere, and the reason why is that, through the years, no matter how much success I achieved, I never lost my faith in God.[9]

Next Franklin was set to do a tour of the United States Virgin Islands and Africa. But before embarking, she told Charles L. Sanders she had to "get something straight about those gigs. I made them give me a contract in which I specify that I won't sing before any segregated audiences. They'll either be totally integrated or all-black. I won't sing for an all-white audience. Black people must be able to come and hear me sing."[10] Her profound commitment to equal rights took on another dimension when she performed with other African-American entertainers in a benefit concert at the Cathedral of Saint John the Divine in New York City. The event was to raise money for aid to drought victims in West Africa.

Franklin was committed to helping people in prison as well. She planned the following year to spend more time entertaining them. "What they get to hear is very limited."[11] She had also started a talent management firm called ALF Productions, and with her sister Carolyn, owned a record label called Do It To It.

From the mid-1960s through the 1970s the world felt the bitterness of political assassinations, anti-war protest marches, and the Vietnam War. America had sent its young men and women to fight in a no-win battle in Southeast Asia. By 1975 the United States had suffered over two hundred thousand casualties. Far from home, American music played a large part in easing the fear and stress of American soldiers. Franklin's recordings were not only "hot" in the United States, but wailed through the Saigon streets of Vietnam. "Bridge Over Troubled Waters," "Respect," and "This Girl Is in Love With You," permeated from cafes, pocket radios, and loudspeakers. Franklin's music was becoming the soundtrack of the era. After the war Franklin said she had heard from many Vietnam vets. "I've had a lot of guys . . . come up to me now and tell me how much my music meant to them over there."[12]

Sad moments continued to interrupt the musical highs in Franklin's life. In 1974 her friend and idol Mahalia Jackson died. At her funeral Franklin sang from the *Songs of Faith* album. Clara Mae Ward also passed away, and once again, Franklin sang from her soul. For Ward she sang "The Day Is Passed and Gone." Franklin had first recorded it when she was fourteen. It was an inspirational hymn that Ward had made famous. These were women Franklin had loved and looked up to when she was a child. Exciting success and sad times seem to prevail during those years.

In 1974 Franklin recorded another blockbuster album, *Let Me In Your Life*. One of the singles, "Until You Come Back to Me," was written by Stevie Wonder. It went gold, and topped the pop charts at Number 3. That same year she won a Grammy for the song "Master of Eyes." And "Ain't Nothing

Like the Real Thing" increased her Grammy totals to an astounding ten. There was more for the reigning "Queen of Soul." Since 1967 she had won eight straight years in the "Best R&B Performance, Female" category. It seemed she would zoom higher and higher.

Chapter 8

COMEBACK!

Franklin appeared to have it all. From the little girl who stood on a chair in her daddy's church to sing, to the "Queen of Soul," she had won the coveted Grammy numerous times. She had certified gold records and albums—more than many popular singers would ever have. She had four healthy sons and was a millionaire many times over. "It's all been wonderful, like a giant, happy dream. I always knew I could sing, but I never suspected it would be anything at all like this."[1]

In concerts, her powerful, sensitive voice and piano playing all come together with high-voltage electricity. During a recent concert she was finishing by going into a "yeah" saying call. The audience came back with "yeah!" Then Franklin started singing "Spirit in the Dark." In her raw and energizing voice a pounding spirit came alive. The audience responded with roaring applause.

But like all things in life, there are ups and downs. Franklin was not immune to low points that can occur in successful careers. In the mid-1970s she entered one of these low spots, and it lasted for five years.

Jerry Wexler, still her producer at Atlantic Records, would not comment on why her records were not doing well. Her pair of album releases, *With Everything I Feel in Me and You*, were among the more disappointing albums of her entire career. Why did this enormously gifted woman's career begin to falter? One critic observed, "Her new album You is a mix of sluggish rhythms, undifferentiated love songs, slim glimmer of elegance and vocal exercise sadly unworthy of Lady Soul."[2]

The press, who had rocketed Franklin to stardom, and *Billboard* magazine, who had once cited her as the top female singer of 1962, now seemingly turned against her. Appearing at the Apollo Theater in Harlem, Franklin chose to wear a spangled lavender costume and a lavender top hat. She sang "Rock-a-Bye Your Baby With a Dixie Melody." One *New Yorker* magazine music critic wrote that her appearance was anything but enthusiastic, noting:

> There was something just slightly defiant about Aretha's manner . . . that this woman, now at ease with herself and her talent, can create an effective stage presence anytime she thinks it useful to do so. She seemed to be announcing that her poise (as well as her talent) is here to stay, and that she reserves the

right to do anything she wants with it. . . . She got the most satisfying sort of applause . . . that comes when no silent space has been allotted for it, and comes because the audience feels it necessary to express a helpless pleasure.[3]

Even though Franklin's career was taking a large share of lumps, she still was invited to appear on several television shows. She was a guest star on *The Muhammad Ali Special, Bob Hope on Campus*, and Johnny Carson's *The Tonight Show*. Tisha Fein finally coaxed her into doing a special television salute titled *Midnight Special*. It was a collection of taped footage of her in church, with her father playing the piano, and then a new segment with gospel songs and talking about growing up. Fein commented afterward, "She was still very shy, but she was real charming."[4]

During this period, despite the lull in her latest recordings, Franklin's personal success got a surprise. It came from Bethune-Cookman College in Florida. In 1904 Mary McLeod Bethune, an African-American educator, started a school with five little girls, $1.50, and faith in God. Its charter was approved and recorded in 1905. The school grew and increased enrollment. A merger with Cookman Institute of Jacksonville, Florida, resulted in 1923 with the founding of Bethune-Cookman College. Years later another African-American woman with a deep faith in God, with the name Aretha Franklin, was awarded an honorary doctor of laws degree from this college.

For eight years Franklin had captured the Grammy awards. In 1976 another African-American singer was the popular choice. A young Natalie Cole broke Franklin's winning streak and garnered two trophies, for "Best New Artist" and her song, "This Will Be." The press heralded Cole as the queen's heiress apparent. Whether or not Franklin had any feelings of jealousy no one knows. However, Natalie Cole suggested to reporters that there were. Noting comparisons in singing styles, one reporter wrote:

> She is, indeed, a child of her times, choosing, instead a robust R&B-based style that demands comparison to Aretha Franklin. The singing strings and fluted lacings of another era have been supplanted by stomping gospel piano chords, whanging guitars and slurred or shouted vocal passages. . . . One can't help but consider what Natalie might have sounded like had she come along before or long after Aretha.[5]

Franklin later remarked, "With respect to maintaining my title as the Queen of Soul, it's second nature to me, and I think, just being myself, the rest will take care of itself."[6]

But even music critics and professional jealousy cannot keep a good woman down. Franklin was gutsy and had a way of always coming back. And this was no time to wallow in failures. Movie producer Curtis Mayfield was making a film called *Sparkle*, and what he wanted was a vibrant soundtrack. He decided to produce an album of eight original songs used in the movie by a celebrated entertainer. This was just what Franklin needed. When she heard the proposal she accepted. The result in 1976 was a gritty urban beat music aimed at the R&B market. A mixed flavor of music ranging from a silky ballad, "Look Into Your Heart," to a red-hot soul sound of "Rock With Me." The results hit the R&B charts at Number 1, and others went on to be Franklin hits.

Franklin's topsy-turvy 1970s took all kinds of spins. Toward the end of the decade not only was Franklin up then down, but her romance with Ken Cunningham was now on the wane. When asked by a reviewer about her problems with men, she paused and reflected, "The best ones are married. . . . You know, when I was in the dressing rooms, touching up my makeup, the other girls were studying men. When I was going onstage and traveling, see, a lot of the best ones got scooped up."[7] Yet love did enter her life again.

The audience at the Circle Star Theater in San Carlos, California, down the peninsula from San Francisco was clapping with the solid rock beat and calling out, "Sing it, Aretha! Sing that song." Then, after a heart-wringing "You Light Up My Life," fans shouted back, "You put Debbie Boone to shame, girl." The "Queen of Soul" grinned and asked, "Do you want to meet someone special?" "Yeah," the crowd roared. "You wanna' meet Glynn?"[8] The rafters shuddered.

Striding down the aisle came Glynn Turman, sporting a white shirt, black slacks, and the off-white cowboy hat he would feel undressed without. He vaulted on stage, took the microphone from Franklin's heavily ringed hand and boomed, "Is my baby doin' it to ya'?" The crowd roared again.

Franklin's brother, Cecil, said, "I've never seen Aretha in better spirits. . . . She's as happy as she's ever been. She's not singing the blues."[9]

In early 1978 Franklin married Turman, a respected actor, twelve years younger than she, and a teacher at Los Angeles' Inner City Repertory Theater. Unlike her first marriage the wedding was elaborate. Reverend Franklin performed the ceremony in his New Bethel Baptist church. A radiant Franklin wore a light beige gown decorated with a seven-foot train and embroidered with seventeen thousand seed pearls that almost knocked out the television cameras of the three networks that covered the event. Twelve bridesmaids attended Franklin. The Four Tops harmonized Stevie Wonder's song "Isn't She Lovely." Sister Carolyn and cousin Brenda sang solos. Turman had twelve groomsmen. The wedding cake, several feet tall, was a work of art.

Turman's longtime friend, actor Lou Gossett, Jr., said, "Glynn and Aretha are two halves of a circle. She's got guts and soul and he's got a disciplined, artistic temperament. They're very close buddies, too, and that's an indication of a long-term relationship."[10]

With her four sons, Clarence, Edward, Teddy, and Kecalf, and Glynn's three children, the family grew overnight. They all moved into a large house in Los Angeles in the valley. Franklin and Turman did have a few differences. Franklin smoked up to two packs of cigarettes a day, and Turman was a vegetarian. Franklin liked to watch the "soaps," and rode in chauffeured limousines, while Turman drove a station wagon. Still he appeared to be just what Franklin needed.

If upside-down was a good definition of Franklin's life during this period, the climax and the worst was yet to come. In June 1979, burglars broke into Reverend Franklin's Detroit home. He was shot twice in the groin. He survived the shooting, but lapsed into a semi-coma from which he never recovered. Five years later he died. Singer and family friend, Mavis Staples said, "The best thing that happened to Aretha was that . . . they kept him alive, because if he had died right then . . . there would have been no more Aretha."[11]

The Reverend Franklin had been not only a guiding light to his daughter, but a teacher and supporter. "He was so special to her," said sister Carolyn. "I think it was something that Aretha couldn't receive or understand from anybody else. She would definitely receive it from her father. . . . I think she adored him."[12]

The 1970s had been a series of triumphs. Deep personal tragedy had also woven its way into her life. The only way for Franklin was up.

Chapter 9

"WHO'S ZOOMIN' WHO?"

The year 1980 started a brand-new decade. Franklin sought out Clive Davis of Arista Records. Her contract with Atlantic had already lapsed. Davis had recently turned two young unknowns, Melissa Manchester and Barry Manilow, into major-league stars. Dionne Warwick had already signed with Arista and scored her biggest selling LP of her career, *Dionne*. "I studied Davis's track record in the trade papers and liked what I saw," said Franklin.[1] She had her attorney call Davis and signed on with this dynamic company.

A movie debut awaited the "Queen of Soul" in the outrageous comedy *The Blues Brothers*. Starring in the title roles were John Belushi and Dan Ackroyd. The story had started as a script on the television show *Saturday Night Live* and blossomed into the film. It also turned into a new recording vehicle for Franklin. Franklin's role, as the owner-operator of a soul restaurant, became one of the high points of the movie. As the plot unfolded, Franklin's husband decides to leave the kitchen and join Belushi and Ackroyd's band. Franklin suggests that he had better "think" before he leaves her. Dressed in a soiled waitress costume, and wearing bedroom slippers, she jumps into a wild, rocking version of "Think." Her sister Carolyn, cousin Brenda, and Margaret Branch—all background singers—are seated on the dining counter's stools, performing a solid soul backup. The movie itself received mixed reviews, but Franklin and the movie's stars were a smash. "Think" and the complete soundtrack album were certified gold.

Yet the media, which could shower entertainers with golden words, were still not forgiving. Franklin's career was not out of the doldrums yet. Verging on signing with Davis, she made her first public appearance in several years on April 25, 1980, at Avery Fisher Hall in New York City. She started off well, introducing Davis as "the eloquent president of my new record company."[2] But *Rolling Stone*'s Stephen Holden sharpened his red pencil. Aretha Franklin's first New York appearance in several years "found the queen of soul [lowercase] floundering at an important crossroads in her career. . . . to judge from her sloppy, distracted performance at Lincoln Center the road back won't be easy."[3]

Holden attacked her voice:

Her incredible voice was in less than top shape; several times she was caught breathless. Worse, she seemed as determined as ever to pursue glitz at the expense of soul. Instead of a crack R&B band, she backed herself with a clattery, second-rate show band that was so poorly rehearsed it could hardly keep time.[4]

And just when the old excitement seemed to return, Franklin returned "to hack away at recent hits by Teddy Pendergrass, the Commodores, Diana Ross, Dionne Warwick, and Michael Jackson." Finally Holden even criticized her dancing as "a clumsy attempt at Las Vegas glamour." The only highlight of the show was her version of "Dr. Feelgood," which brought a standing ovation. Holden concluded "the evening could have been saved. Instead it petered out in the trappings of a tacky burlesque show."[5]

Franklin had made it to the top of the music world with not only a passionate energy, but with talent, guts, and determination. Being down did not mean success was behind her. In the beginning of the 1980s Franklin sang the powerful spiritual "Amazing Grace" and "My Shining Hour" as part of a variety performance for the Queen of England. Then came her hit "Can't Turn You Loose." It was nominated for a Grammy in the R&B Vocal Performance, Female. She did not win an award that year. Nevertheless she had been nominated, and things were looking up for the "Queen of Soul."

Her next album brought back the old sizzle and hot kick that originally had sent her to the top. *Love All the Hard Way* in 1981 broke Number 36 on *Billboard*'s album charts, becoming her first LP to score in the top forty in six years. Two years later her vocal arrangement of "Hold On I'm Comin'" took a dramatic leap forward. For it, she won the Best R&B Vocal Performance, Female. Franklin had garnered her eleventh Grammy. And now the honors just kept coming. Her third album for Arista, the ultra-hot *Jump To It*, produced by Luther Vandross, brought back the coveted gold.

Franklin was back on top! Her recordings were cracking the charts. She had a good marriage with Glynn Turman, and lived on a California estate. The only sad part was that her father remained in a coma in Detroit.

In 1983 she cut another winning album with Luther Vandross titled *Get It Right*. Next came a ribbon cutting for the first Los Angeles Street Scene Festival. Rave notices for concert and television appearances rounded out Franklin's next several years. Her career was reaching astounding heights and pointed in only an upward position. Still a happy marriage did not seem to be in Franklin's life. Suddenly, in that same year, she left Turman and the big California estate and headed home to Detroit. She never gave sufficient reason for her failed relationship. Instead, Franklin respectfully kept personal matters to herself, and the reasons for the divorce remain a mystery.

If men were a jinx in Franklin's life, music certainly was not. She was hitting the highs with her recordings, her fans adored her, and she was home in Detroit. Yet another sad note was to be heard. On July 27, 1984, her father, the

Reverend Clarence LaVaughn Franklin, age sixty-nine, died. He had never regained consciousness after being shot by a burglar five years earlier. *Newsweek* magazine reported:

> A fiery preacher whose powerful, mournful sermons packed his church and drew listeners nationwide on radio broadcasts for thirty years had emerged as an early leader of the civil rights movement in Detroit, leading 100,000 people in a freedom march down Woodward Avenue in June 1963 with the Reverend Martin Luther King, Jr.[6]

Reverend Jesse Jackson delivered the eulogy as more than ten thousand people crowded into the church.

Reverend Franklin's death had a profound impact on his daughter and the album she was cutting. Narada Michael Walden, her producer, said, "There was a new verve in her voice. As if she'd been set free."[7] When Arista's Clive Davis finally gave Walden the nod to write for Franklin, an all-time success was about to erupt. Franklin said about Walden:

> He knows his music very well. He knows what he's going to do when he gets there, and yet it's not a straight-ahead work kind of thing. It's very relaxed. We kid around a lot, we talk about a lot of different things, I get the best ribs [barbecued spareribs] in town![8]

The music that she and Walden put together took away any previous misgivings. "Freeway of Love" became her first smash hit in more than ten years, and her twentieth single to reach No. 1 on the soul charts—an unprecedented feat approached only by James Brown. Her voice was in full flight, blessed with that remarkable range. The 1985 album, *Who's Zoomin' Who?*, her twenty-second, zoomed into the top 20. Clarence Clemons (on loan from Bruce Springsteen's E Street Band) wailed his saxophone, and a cameo solo by rock guitarist Carlos Santana completed the success. The music critics hailed her comeback. *Newsweek* wrote, "Above all, there's that voice. It flutters and floats, snaps and shouts, cries and laughs. Welcome back, 'Lady Soul.'"[9] *People* magazine reported, "The sexually suggestive 'Freeway of Love' had sold a heady 700,000 copies since its release . . . and *Who's Zoomin' Who?* had zoomed into the top 20, propelled by a hammer-hard dance beat and Aretha's own typically intense gospel-style vocals."[10] *Jet* magazine reported that "[Franklin, who] has waxed more million-selling hit songs than any other female artist in the history of the recording industry, . . . is riding the crest of a new wave of popularity with a new hit album *Who's Zoomin' Who?*" With Franklin zooming down the freeway of media love and success, she told *Jet,* "I don't think my music has changed. It's basically the same—maybe a little more commercially-oriented."[11]

In 1985, while Franklin basked in the brilliant glow of recovery and the favor of old and new fans, a group of concerned parents were seeking to have labels put on records with sexually explicit lyrics. Franklin was aware of this, and told *Jet* that her music was not affected by their actions. "I'm a parent and I care about the kind of music they listen to. I agree with Smokey Robinson, who said, that we must be kind to growing minds."[12]

The sidebar story alongside a *Newsweek* music review did not mention Franklin nor her music. It did note that "beginning this fall 19 major record companies will identify selected albums and cassettes with a warning—PARENTAL GUIDANCE: Explicit Lyrics. 'We're saying a line of decency has been crossed,'" said Susan Baker of the Parents' Music Resources Center in Washington, and wife of then Treasury Secretary James A. Baker.[13]

Newsweek seemed to love the controversy, and countered the sidebar story with a powerful review of Franklin's latest work:

> [Franklin's] electrifying performance of "Sweet Bitter Love" makes the title's cruel paradox seem like God's only revealed truth. In the midst of the dance track, "Another Night," she takes the word 'laughing' and makes it sound like it has been kissed with death. And on "Integrity," a blunt feminist lyric wrapped in a sleek pop song, . . . [Franklin] fires off the words like bullets.[14]

Franklin always welcomed record sales and high marks on the charts, but not the media scrutiny they inevitably created. She now lives in a big white colonial home tucked away on three acres in posh Bloomfield Hills, Michigan—a suburb of Detroit. She shies away from talking about her marriages and the death of her father. She is the kind of superstar who arrives at work in a limousine, wearing a mink coat over a T-shirt and jeans. At home she likes to watch soap operas and cook collard greens, fried chicken, or a plate of barbecue ribs. And she likes to describe herself as "just the nice lady who lives next door."[15]

Chapter 10

SPANNING THE AGE GAP

F reeway of Love" was a departure from previous single records for Franklin. "I wanted something that kids would enjoy, something that would span the age gap, but not leave older fans behind. The soul is still there."[1]

Approaching the zenith of her long career, "Freeway of Love" won a Grammy in 1985 for Best R&B Performance, Female. Accolades followed in multitudes. The state of Michigan saluted Franklin on her twenty-fifth year in show business and declared her voice a "natural resource." "Aretha Franklin Appreciation Day" was officially proclaimed by Michigan Governor James J. Blanchard on May 23, 1985, and the Michigan state senate and house of representatives entered the acknowledgment and a resolution into the record.

"Freeway of Love" was later featured on her first videocassette, *Aretha: Ridin' on the Freeway*, released in 1987. It became an official Detroit roadway, July 24, 1985, when a section of Washington Boulevard at State Street was renamed. Franklin was now not only riding in her pink Cadillac on the "Freeway of Love," but was in demand to do commercials as well. She sang the jingle "Coke Is It" for Coca-Cola® in 1985, and the "Aren't You Glad" song for Dial® soap. The next year she performed in an hour-long television special, *Aretha*.

In 1987 the fame and awards of Franklin began a never-ending swell. During the first half of the decade, Franklin was selected as the first female inductee into the Rock and Roll Hall of Fame. Aside from being in her mid-forties, the winner of fifteen Grammies, twenty-four gold records and albums, and one platinum album, she now had back-to-back hits. Franklin had returned to where she was twenty years ago: sitting on top of the charts.

"One Lord One Faith, One Baptism" was such an event that it made the wire services. *Ms.* magazine reporter Bonnie Allen wrote:

> My guess is that if an atheist was ever going to find God, it would have been as part of that sweating, grid-locked audience spurred on by a 100-voice choir, and taken to the limit by the Franklin Sisters [Erma, Carolyn, and cousin Brenda], Mavis Staples of the Staples Singers, and God's great gift, Aretha, making a joyful noise unto the Lord for three nights. If there is a roof still on that church some people would take it as proof that God makes miracles.[2]

"One Lord One Faith, One Baptism," was an all-star revival meeting captured on tape during three hot and humid nights at the New Bethel Baptist Church. As the first song, "Jesus Is the Light of the World" began, the choir marched down the aisle holding candles. The two-record set is a deeply inspired religious service with music and spoken word. Franklin's three magnificent solos were "Walkin' the Light," "Ave Maria," and "The Lord's Prayer." Reverend Jesse Jackson, Reverend Jaspar Williams, Franklin's brother Reverend Cecil Franklin, and Reverend Donald Parson, of the Mount Calvary Baptist Church in Chicago, were the speakers. Four thousand fans sat through the hot (both music and temperature) event, cooling themselves with cardboard fans. As a personal fulfillment, Franklin had produced and coordinated the spectacular event.[3]

When the thirteenth annual Grammy awards were presented in March 1988, it was Franklin who took her thirteenth and fourteenth Grammies, becoming the female artist with the greatest number of awards in any musical category. "I Knew You Were Waiting for Me," won as the Best R&B Performance by a Duo, Group or Chorus, and her album *Aretha* won the Best R&B Vocal Performance, Female. Despite her successes, tragedy never seemed to leave Franklin's side. A month after this last honor, her sister Carolyn Franklin died of cancer.

Franklin's ninth album for Arista Records, recorded in 1992, continued a winning streak. Following her funky remake of Sly Stone's "Everyday People" and the album release of *What You See Is What You Sweat*, she had a slew of live performances.

During the next six years Franklin did occasional shows in the Midwest and on the East Coast. On the West Coast she was booked for a four-day stint at Las Vegas' Caesar's Palace, three nights at the Greek Theater in Los Angeles, and television appearances on *The Arsenio Hall Show and Murphy Brown*. Franklin and Candice Bergen (Murphy Brown) joined in a rollicking rendition of "You Make Me Feel Like a Natural Woman."

A number of top producers contributed to her ninth album with Arista, including Luther Vandross and Burt Bacharach. Franklin told David Nathan of *Billboard* magazine, "I'm extremely happy with the album. . . . I love the versatility of the selections and as much as anyone can put on one album, I really think the record reflects me." She added that two of the songs she penned for the album were "personal testimonies."[4]

"I wrote 'You Can't Take Me for Granted' with a very special man in mind, someone with whom I had a very long standing relationship. . . . In essence, the song is saying although your picture's in my locket, I'm not in your back pocket."[5] She said of composer Sly Stone's "Everyday People"— also on video—"I felt it was a good way to introduce his music to the young members of the audience." Franklin was also taking classes to overcome a fear of flying that developed after a turbulent plane ride in the 1980s, since she was planning several overseas tours. "Performing is something I never tire of. It's lost none of its magic for me."[6]

As Franklin matured in years, she expanded her honors and community involvement. In May 1992 Franklin received a special Lifetime Achievement Award at the third annual

Rhythm & Blues Foundation Pioneer Awards in New York City. Ten other Pioneer Awards were presented as well. The gala presentation concluded with an all-star jam, which featured singer Carla Thomas (daughter of award winner Rufus Thomas), the Uptown Horn, drummer Tyrone "Krusher" Green, bassist Wilbur Baskin, and guitarist/band leader Danny Draher.

At President Bill Clinton's 1993 Inaugural Gala, Franklin gave one of the finest performances of her life, singing the beautiful and powerful "I Dreamed a Dream." Softly she told the audience, "I always supported Dr. King and I believe in his dream."[7]

In the past Franklin had lent her support to other charities, and when asked to help raise funds for cultural support she starred in a Carnegie Hall concert for the Joffrey Ballet. Nancy Reagan, wife of President Ronald Reagan, was the honorary national chairperson. When the National Alliance for Breast Cancer Organization requested her voice, Franklin was there. In 1994 she, Tina Turner, Annie Lennox, Carly Simon, Melissa Etheridge, and Amy Grant were featured on *Women for Women*, a CD and cassette benefitting the cancer organization. The Mercury Records release was a compilation of prerecorded songs that also featured Lisa Stansfield, Olete Adams, Kathy Mattea, Cathy Dennis, Sheryl Crow, Taylor Dane, Julia Fordham, and Vanessa Williams.

Franklin also released her autobiography, *Aretha: From These Roots* in 1999. In addition to the book, Franklin had a number of projects in the works—a family album with her sons ("If they don't sing, they play an instrument") to be recorded on her own label, World Class Records, and a cooking video and her album *Live at Carnegie Hall.*[8]

Still, honors and stellar performances continue—and in extraordinary proportions. In the White House Rose Garden, Franklin again sang for President Clinton, mellowing him and the audience with "Look to the Rainbow" and "Tomorrowland." No doubt, greatest of all her achievements, was to be one of five honored by the Kennedy Center Honors. In December 1994, the capital paid tribute to "five American artistic legends:" actor Kirk Douglas, folk musician Pete Seeger, composer Morton Gould, Broadway director Harold Prince, and the "Queen of Soul," Aretha Franklin.

Prior to the event a swirl of activity and people met over fine wine and food at some of Washington's grandest sites, and a White House reception hosted by President Clinton. Aaron Nathans of the *Los Angeles Times* reported, "Arriving at the Saturday dinner in a blazing red dress, Franklin said receiving the award was 'the pinnacle of my career.' At fifty-two, she is the youngest person ever chosen for the award."[9]

Jazz pianist Herbie Hancock, toasting Franklin, recalled hearing her play piano at the Adams Theater in Los Angeles. "She had a wonderful swinging style, bluesy in nature—it sounded fabulous. And then, she sang . . . My, my, my. What came out filled the entire room, the entire planet, and filled everybody's life."[10]

Franklin was saluted at the Kennedy Center by the Four Tops, Patti LaBelle, and the choir from her father's New Bethel Baptist Church in Detroit.

She returned to Washington, D.C., in January 2009 to perform "My Country 'Tis of Thee," during the inaugural ceremony for President Barack Obama. In 2012, Franklin was inducted into the GMA Gospel Music Hall of Fame. And in 2014, she was awarded an honorary doctorate by Harvard University for her contributions to music.

It had been a long journey from the platform of the New Bethel Baptist Church in Detroit, where the young girl stood on a chair to sing. The press had praised her, and then with vengeance, ripped into her music performances and personal life. There were appearances in noisy, smoke-filled nightclubs, gilded and velvet-draped theaters, and endless bus rides across the country—and there were her fans.

Mark Jacobson was a porter in a bus terminal when he heard Franklin explode with "Respect:"

Is there anyone who has ever gotten tired of "Respect"? Ain't no way. Years ago, before Newark, before King got shot, there was something in Aretha's voice that said hope really was alive, that anything was possible. Now, in much less expansive times, Aretha remains a constant, a lodestone. The mere existence of a voice like hers is a revelation, an affirmation, proof of life beyond the everyday.[11]

CHRONOLOGY

1942—Born in Memphis, Tennessee, on March 25.

1955—Makes first public appearance singing in her father's church choir.

1956—Leaves school to tour with her father.

1957—First son, Clarence Franklin, is born.

1959—Second son, Edward Franklin, is born.

1960—Signs recording contract with Columbia Records.

1961—Marries Ted White; third son, Teddy White, Jr., is born.

1966—Signs recording contract with Atlantic Records.

1967—Wins first Grammy Award, for Best R&B Recording, with "Respect."

1968—The city of Detroit, Michigan, declares "Aretha Franklin Day;" sings at the funeral of Martin Luther King, Jr.; divorces Ted White.

1970—Fourth son, Kecalf Franklin, is born.

1974—Sings at the funeral of Mahalia Jackson.

1975—Receives an honorary doctorate from Bethune-Cookman College.

1978—Marries Glynn Turman.

1980—Appears in *The Blues Brothers* movie with John Belushi and Dan Ackroyd; sings a command performance for Queen Elizabeth II.

1984—Franklin's father, Reverend Clarence LaVaughn Franklin, dies.

1985—The city of Lansing, Michigan, declares Franklin's voice "a natural resource"; sings commercial jingles for Dial® soap and Coca-Cola®; appears in television special, *Aretha*.

1987—Becomes the first woman inducted into the Rock & Roll Hall of Fame.

1988—Wins fifteenth Grammy Award for "One Lord, One Faith, One Baptism."

1992—Receives Lifetime Achievement Award.

1993—Sings at President Bill Clinton's inaugural ball.

1994—Sings for President Bill Clinton in the White House Rose Garden.

1995—Appears in television special, *Aretha Coming Home*.

1998—Has a top 40 hit with the song "A Rose Is Still a Rose."

2009—Performs at inaugural ceremony for President Barack Obama.

2012—Inducted into the GMA Gospel Music Hall of Fame.

2014—Receives an honorary doctorate degree from Harvard University for her contributions to music.

SELECTED DISCOGRAPHY

Albums

Songs of Faith. (Chess, 1956.)

The Electrifying Aretha Franklin. (Columbia, 1962.)

Laughing on the Outside. (Columbia, 1963.)

Unforgettable—A Tribute to Dinah Washington. (Columbia, 1964.)

Runnin' Out of Fools. (Columbia, 1964.)

Yeah!!! (Columbia, 1965.)

Soul Sister. (Columbia, 1965.)

Take a Look. (Columbia, 1967.)

Aretha Arrives. (Columbia, 1967.)

Aretha Franklin's Greatest Hits. (Columbia, 1967.)

I Never Loved a Man the Way I Love You. (Atlantic, 1967.)

Lady Soul. (Atlantic, 1968.)

Aretha in Paris. (Atlantic, 1968.)

This Girl's in Love With You. (Atlantic, 1970.)

Aretha Live at the Fillmore West. (Atlantic, 1971.)

Young, Gifted and Black. (Atlantic, 1972.)

Amazing Grace. (Atlantic, 1972.)

Today I Sing the Blues. (Columbia, 1973.)

With Everything I Feel in Me. (Atlantic, 1974.)

You. (Atlantic, 1975.)

Ten Years of Gold. (Atlantic, 1976.)

The Blues Brothers. (Atlantic, 1980.)

Love All the Hard Way. (Atlantic, 1981.)

Jump To It. (Arista, 1982.)

Back Where I Belong. (Motown, 1983.)

Aretha's Jazz. (Atlantic, 1984.)

Who's Zoomin' Who? (Arista, 1985.)

Aretha Sings the Blues. (Columbia, 1985.)

After Hours. (Columbia, 1987.)

I'm Gonna Git You Sucka!. (Arista, 1988.)

Indestructible. (Arista, 1988.)

What You See Is What You Sweat. (Arista, 1992.)

Live at Carnegie Hall. (World Class Records, 1995.)

A Rose Is Still a Rose. (Arista, 1998.)

So Damn Happy. (Arista, 2003.)

A Woman Falling Out of Love (Aretha's Records, 2011.)

Singles

"Today I Sing the Blues" (Columbia, 1960.)

"Precious Lord (Part One)/Precious Lord (Part Two)" (Chess, 1964.)

"Respect"/"Dr. Feelgood" (Atlantic, 1967.)

"Chain of Fools" (Atlantic, 1967.)

"Think"/"You Send Me" (Atlantic, 1967.)

"Ain't No Way" (Atlantic, 1968.)

"Eleanor Rigby" (Atlantic, 1969.)

"Bridge Over Troubled Waters"/"Brand New Me" (Atlantic, 1971.)

"Jump" (Atlantic, 1976.)

"Jump To It" (Arista, 1983.)

"Freeway of Love" (Arista, 1985.)

"Who's Zoomin' Who?" (Arista, 1985.)

"Oh Happy Day" (duet with Mavis Staples, Arista, 1987.)

"Through the Storm" (duet with Elton John, Arista, 1989.)

"It Isn't, It Wasn't, It Ain't Never Gonna Be" (duet with Whitney Houston, Arista, 1989.)

"Willing to Forgive" (Arista, 1994)

"A Rose Is Still a Rose" (Arista, 1998.)

"Wonderful" (Arista, 2003.)

"How Long I've Been Waiting" (Aretha's Records, 2011.)

CHAPTER NOTES

Chapter 1. Rocking in the Rose Garden

1. James T. Jones, IV, "Soul of the Queen," *Vanity Fair*, March 1994, p. 58.

2. Mary Ann French, "House Full of Soul," *Washington Post*, June 21, 1994, pp. E1–E2.

3. James T. Jones, IV, "Franklin's Encore for the Clintons," *USA Today*, June 21, 1994, p. D2.

4. French, p. E2.

5. Ibid.

6. Jones, "Franklin's Encore for the Clintons," p. D2.

7. Jones, "Soul of the Queen," p. 70.

8. Ibid., p. 58.

Chapter 2. Back to the Beginning

1. Mahalia Jackson with Evan McLeod Wylie, *Movin' on Up* (New York: Hawthorn Books, 1966), p. 212.

2. James T. Jones, IV, "Soul of the Queen," *Vanity Fair*, March 1994, pp. 60–64.

3. Mark Bego, *Aretha Franklin: The Queen of Soul* (New York: St. Martin's Press, 1989), p. 12.

4. Jones, p. 64.

5. "Singing for Sinners," *Newsweek*, September 2, 1957, p. 86.

6. Ibid.

7. Ibid.

8. James T. Olson, *Aretha Franklin* (Mankato, Minn.: Creative Education, 1975), p. 10.

9. Edward J. Boyer, "The Soulful Legacy of Sam Cooke," *Los Angeles Times*, December 23, 1994, p. 1.

10. Bego, p. 15.

11. "Singing for Sinners," p. 86.

12. Olson, p. 10.

13. Ibid.

14. Ibid.

15. Bego, p. 16.

Chapter 3. "Precious Lord"

1. Mark Bego, *Aretha Franklin: The Queen of Soul* (New York: St. Martin's Press, 1989), p. 20.

2."Poverty and Discrimination," *World Book Encyclopedia* (Chicago: Field Enterprise Education Corporation, 1994), Vol. 20, p. 191.

3. Jim Haskins, *Queen of the Blues* (New York: William Morrow and Company, 1987), p. 141.

4. John Hammond with Irving Townsend, *John Hammond on Record* (New York: Summit Books, 1977), p. 123.

5. Ibid.

6. Edward J. Boyer, "The Soulful Legacy of Sam Cooke," *Los Angeles Times*, December 23, 1994, p. 27.

7. Bego, p. 24.

8. Ibid., p. 29.

9. Laura B. Randolph, "Aretha Talks About Men, Marriage, Music and Motherhood," *Ebony*, April 1995, pp. 30–32.

10. Ibid., p. 29.

11. Hammond and Townsend, p. 346.

Chapter 4. Making It on Record

1. Laurraine Goreau, *Just Mahalia Baby* (Waco, Tex.: Word Books, 1975), p. 280.

2. Mark Bego, *Aretha Franklin: The Queen of Soul* (New York: St. Martin's Press, 1989), p. 47.

3. John Hammond with Irving Townsend, *John Hammond on Record* (New York: Summit Books, 1977), p. 348.

4. Paul D. Zimmerman, "Over the Rainbow," *Newsweek*, August 21, 1967, p. 70.

5. Hammond and Townsend, p. 349.

6. James T. Olson, *Aretha Franklin* (Mankato, Minn.: Creative Education, 1975), pp. 11–12.

7. James T. Jones, IV, "Soul of the Queen," *Vanity Fair*, March 1994, p. 66.

8. Bego, p. 61.

9. Jerry Wexler and David Ritz, *Rhythm and the Blues* (New York: Alfred A. Knopf, 1993), p. 212.

10. Ibid.

11. Ibid.

12. Ibid., p. 213.

13. Pete Howard, "CD News," *Rolling Stone*, September 3, 1992, p. 50.

14. Bego, p. 59.

15. Olson, p. 17.

16. Jones, p. 68.

Chapter 5. The Civil Rights Movement

1. Flip Schulke and Penelope McPhee, *King Remembered* (New York: W.W. Norton & Company, 1986), p. 144.

2. Aretha Franklin, speaking on *Aretha Franklin Coming Home*, television program, The Disney Channel, March 25, 1994.

3. Patricia C. McKissack, *Jesse Jackson* (New York: Scholastic, Inc., 1989), pp. 20–23.

4. Ibid., p. 24.

5. Ibid., p. 28.

6. Ibid., pp. 34–35.

7. Ibid., pp. 42–43.

8. Ibid., p. 46.

9. Homer Bigart, "High and Lowly Join in Last Tribute to Rights Champion," *The New York Times*, April 9, 1968, pp. 1–2.

10. Ibid.

11. Ibid.

12. Albert Goldman, "Aretha Franklin: She Makes Salvation Seem Erotic," *The New York Times*, March 31, 1968, p. 33.

Chapter 6. Has It Got Soul?

1. "Lady Soul: Singing It Like It Is," *Time*, June 28, 1968, p. 62.

2. Ibid., p. 62.

3. James T. Olson, *Aretha Franklin* (Mankato, Minn.: Creative Education, 1975), pp. 14–17.

4. "Lady Soul: Singing It Like It Is," p. 62.

5. "Singers," *Time*, January 5, 1968, p. 48.

6. Olson, p. 19.

7. "Singers," p. 48.

8. Olson, p. 17.

9. James T. Jones, IV, "Soul of the Queen," *Vanity Fair*, March 1994, p. 68.

10. Ibid., p. 70.

11. Jerry Wexler and David Ritz, *Rhythm and the Blues* (New York: Alfred A. Knopf, 1993), p. 208.

12. Mark Bego, *Aretha Franklin: The Queen of Soul* (New York: St. Martin's Press, 1989), p. 119.

13. Wexler and Ritz, p. 245.

14. Ibid.

15. Ibid.

16. Ibid.

Chapter 7. "Amazing Grace"

1. Jerry Wexler and David Ritz, *Rhythm and the Blues* (New York: Alfred A. Knopf, 1993), p. 247.

2. Ibid., p. 247.

3. Mark Bego, *Aretha Franklin: The Queen of Soul* (New York: St. Martin's Press, 1989), p. 145.

4. Wexler and Ritz, p. 246.

5. Edward J. Boyer, "The Soulful Legacy of Sam Cooke," *Los Angeles Times*, December 23, 1994, p. 1.

6. Wexler and Ritz, p. 246.

7. Bego, p. 149.

8. Ibid., p. 153.

9. Charles L. Sanders, "Aretha: A Close-up Look at Sister Superstar," *Ebony*, December 1971, p. 134.

10. Ibid.

11. Ibid.

12. Bego, p. 136.

Chapter 8. Comeback!

1. James T. Olson, *Aretha Franklin* (Mankato, Minn.: Creative Education, 1975), p. 26.

2. Peter Guralnick, "Aretha Franklin's Supper Club Soul," *Rolling Stone*, January 1, 1976, p. 60.

3. "The Talk of the Town," *The New Yorker*, March 25, 1974, pp. 31–32.

4. Mark Bego, *Aretha Franklin: The Queen of Soul* (New York: St. Martin's Press, 1989), p. 166.

5. Phyl Garland, untitled article, *Ebony*, December 1975, p. 7.

6. James T. Jones, IV, "Soul of the Queen," *Vanity Fair*, March 1994, p. 73.

7. Ibid., p. 70.

8. Lois Armstrong, "Lady Soul Aretha Franklin Only Sings the Blues Onstage, Now That She's Wed Glynn Turman," *People Weekly*, November 6, 1978, p. 79.

9. Ibid., p. 80.

10. Ibid., p. 82.

11. Jones, p. 70.

12. Ibid.

Chapter 9. "Who's Zoomin' Who?"

1. Aretha Franklin, speaking on *Aretha Franklin Coming Home*, television program, The Disney Channel, March 25, 1994.

2. Stephen Holden, "Aretha's Hard Road Back," *Rolling Stone*, June 26, 1980, p. 92.

3. Ibid.

4. Ibid.

5. Ibid.

6. "Transition," *Newsweek*, August 13, 1984, p. 67.

7. Jim Miller and Linda Tibbetts, "Cruising the Freeway of Love," *Newsweek*, August 26, 1985, p. 69.

8. Mark Bego, *Aretha Franklin: The Queen of Soul* (New York: St. Martin's Press, 1989), p. 225.

9. Ibid.

10. Roger Wolmuth and Julie Greenwalt, "A Bloomin' *Zoomin'* Helps Aretha Franklin Past Her Dad's Death and a Career-Threatening Phobia," *People Weekly*, October 14, 1985, p. 55.

11. Ibid.

12. "Aretha Franklin: Zooming Down Freeway of Love and Success," *Jet*, November 4, 1985, p. 57.

13. "Next: R-Rated Record Albums?" *Newsweek*, August 26, 1985, p. 69.

14. Miller and Tibbetts, p. 69.

15. Ibid.

Chapter 10. Spanning the Age Gap

1. Jim Miller and Linda Tibbetts, "Cruising the Freeway of Love," *Newsweek*, August 26, 1985, p. 69.

2. Bonnie Allen, "God's Great Gift, Aretha," *Ms.*, December 1987, p. 77.

3. Aretha Franklin, speaking on *Aretha Franklin Coming Home*, television program, The Disney Channel, March 25, 1994.

4. Ibid.

5. Ibid.

6. David Nathan, "Aretha Franklin Is in the Public Eye," *Billboard*, August 3, 1991, p. 19.

7. Aretha Franklin, *President Clinton's Inaugural Gala*, television program, March 1995.

8. Laura B. Randolph, "Aretha Talks About Men, Marriage, Music and Motherhood," *Ebony*, April 1995, p. 32.

9. Aaron Nathans, "Five American Legends of Art Are Honored," *Los Angeles Times*, December 5, 1994, p. A16.

10. Ibid.

11. Mark Jacobson, "Aretha," *Esquire*, January 1989, p. 102.

FURTHER READING

Books

Anniss, Matt. *The Story of Soul and R&B*. North Mankato, Minn.: Smart Apple Media, 2013.

Carroll, Jillian. *Aretha Franklin*. North Mankato, Minn.: Heinemann-Raintree, 2003.

Handyside, Christopher. *Soul and R&B*. North Mankato, Minn.: Heinemann-Raintree, 2005.

McAvoy, Jim. *Aretha Franklin*. New York: Chelsea House Publishers, 2001.

Rivera, Ursula. *Aretha Franklin*. New York: Rosen Publishers, 2002.

Wagner, Heather Lehr. *Aretha Franklin: Singer*. New York: Chelsea House Publishers, 2010.

INDEX

PEACHTREE CITY LIBRARY
201 Willowbend Road
Peachtree City, GA 30269-1623
Phone 770-631-2520
Fax 770-631-2522

PEACHTREE CITY

PLAN TO STAY™

PEACHTREE CITY LIBRARY
201 Willowbend Road
Peachtree City, GA 30269-1623
Phone: 770-631-2520
Fax: 770-631-2522